HOME
IN THE
COUNTRY

For Efi

THIS IS A CARLTON BOOK

Design copyright © 1999 Carlton Books Limited
Text copyright © 1999 Alison Cork
Pictures © 1999 Carlton Books Limited

This edition published by Carlton Books Limited 1999
20 St Anne's Court
Wardour Street
London
W1V 3AW

A CIP catalogue for this book is available from the British Library.

ISBN 1 85868 905 8

Editorial manager: Penny Simpson
Senior art editor: Tim Brown
Art editor: Adam Wright
Design: Wayne Humphries
Cover design: Paul Oakley and Trevor Newman
Production: Garry Lewis
Photography: Peter Story and Laurie Evans
Styling: Shannon Beare and Roísín Nield
Home economists: Lucy Miller, Barbara Birch and Mari Williams
Craft advisor: Sylvia Bird

Home in the Country is a Carlton production for ITV,
produced and directed by Howard Perks.

Printed in the United Kingdom by Butler & Tanner Limited.

HOME
IN THE
COUNTRY

Alison Cork

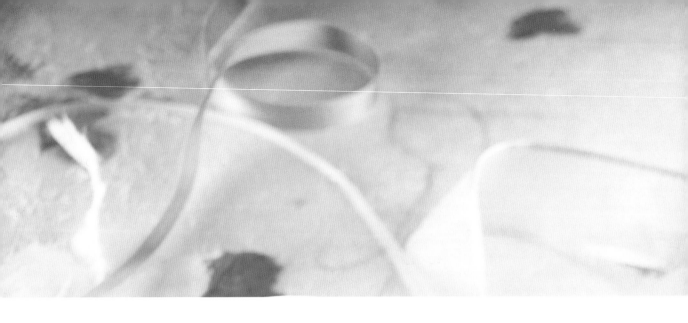

contents

Introduction

There are few sayings truer than "home is where the heart is". The word "home" conjures up all sorts of emotions and, for most of us, represents far more than just four walls. To me, home means safety, warmth, food, comfort and beauty. In fact, all the good things in life, and that is what *Home in the Country* is all about.

Picture an idyllic house nestling in a classic country garden and imagine the wonderful smell of baking wafting out of the kitchen. We've nearly all had that dream of a perfect rural existence, myself included, but it wasn't until my mid-twenties that I actually managed to move to the country. Ironically, the reality of living in the countryside is that it can be very hard work, but it is also inspiring, and it is that inspiration I always try to recreate in my television programmes.

Throughout the seasons, the countryside weaves its own special tapestry of colours, textures and tastes. It might be the scent of a misty autumn morning, the ripe fruits of the late summer garden or the crisp colours of spring; whatever the inspiration, it always seems to find its way into my recipes, ideas for the garden or decorative projects for the interior. And all my ideas have one simple aim – to make a house into a real home, wherever it might be.

As we approach the millennium there is undoubtedly a sense of great excitement, but also one of uncertainty. Nobody really knows what the year 2000 will bring. But the one area we can have control over is our private space, our home, which has consequently become an even more important part of our life. "Staying in" is the new "going out" and the art of homemaking is once again relevant to our lifestyle.

Of course, that doesn't mean we all have limitless time to spend at or on our home. On the contrary, it means that the time we do spend has to pay generous dividends, and I always try to weigh up the effort

versus the reward when thinking up a new recipe or decorative idea. If it isn't a ten-minute miracle, it often doesn't make the grade!

Christmas, however, is a rather special time of year. I find myself seeking labour-saving ideas for the more mundane jobs, but I also want to take time to enjoy decorating the house. And, of course, it's a season for children, who have to be catered for in every respect. So I do allow a bit of leeway when it comes to projects for the festive season, because I know that there are many people who want to spend a little extra time on their preparations.

However you use this book, I hope that you find it both helpful and inspirational. It seems especially appropriate that as we stand on the verge of a new millennium, *Home in the Country* offers a blend of ideas inspired both by the past and present. In this ever-changing world our home is one of the few constants, and for that reason alone I know that the art of homemaking will continue to be practised and appreciated.

Alison Cork

Cards

Cards are one of the more personal aspects of Christmas, an opportunity to send the season's greetings, to say something you couldn't say out loud, to put right a wrong, or simply to renew old acquaintances. They are a very intimate means of communication, so what better way to get the right message across than to make the cards yourself. Christmas can be so highly commercialised that anything handmade comes as a breath of fresh air – it is also much more likely to be remembered and appreciated by the recipient.

Stained glass cards

A most realistic stained glass effect card and a great idea for children to try. Use as many paints as you can, to create a real kaleidoscope of colour.

1. Cut a piece of acetate slightly larger than the window of the card and stick it to the back of the window with double-sided sticky tape.

2. Draw your picture or pattern on a piece of paper the same size or smaller than your window. Stained glass window designs work well and are very appropriate for Christmas.

3. Lie the piece of paper underneath the acetate window and trace the pattern on to the acetate with your tube of relief paint. Make sure that there are no gaps in your lines, otherwise the paint will seep through. Allow the paint to dry (this will take about 20 minutes; if you are in a hurry use a hairdryer).

4. When the relief paint is completely dry, fill in the outline with glass paints. Use either

MATERIALS:

READY-MADE WINDOW CARDS (FROM STATIONERS OR HABERDASHERY DEPARTMENTS)
SEVERAL SHEETS OF ACETATE (FROM STATIONERS)
SCISSORS
DOUBLE-SIDED STICKY TAPE
PLAIN PAPER
BALLPOINT PEN
RELIEF PAINT, AVAILABLE IN TUBES FROM ART SHOPS
SOLVENT- OR WATER-BASED PAINT IN VARIOUS COLOURS OF YOUR CHOICE
SELECTION OF FINE PAINTBRUSHES

solvent-based or water-based paints but don't mix the two or the colours will go cloudy.

5. Leave the card to dry overnight.

Scented cards

By the time Christmas comes, summer is a very distant memory. I love these cards because they evoke the wonderful perfume of sunny days in the garden – a fragrant surprise on a cold winter's day.

1. Cut out your basic card.

2. Cut a square of netting to act as a pocket for the rosebuds. You can use muslin, but netting is particularly suitable as it does not fray and is sufficiently transparent for the detail of the rosebuds to show through. If you want to create an "antique look" net, just soak it in water infused with a teabag and leave to dry.

3. Glue the netting on to the card on three sides only, leaving the top of the pocket open.

4. Insert the rosebuds into the pocket, adding a few drops of essential oil for extra perfume.

5. You can make these cards as ornate or simple

MATERIALS:

SHEETS OF CARD IN YOUR CHOICE OF COLOURS
SCISSORS
FINE NETTING – CURTAIN NETTING WILL DO
ALL-PURPOSE CRAFT GLUE
SMALL DRIED ROSEBUDS
ROSE ESSENTIAL OIL

as you like, but I think that the best effect is created by using high-quality paper and letting the beauty of the rosebuds show through. You could adapt them for Valentine's Day by using red card and cutting a heart-shaped net pocket.

We can get a bit overwhelmed by gold and silver at Christmas, so I like to balance that with ideas inspired by the natural hues and textures of the countryside. These cards are quite charming and have that luxury handmade feel to them. You could also frame them to make really beautiful pictures.

Cards *from the* Countryside

MATERIALS:

SELECTION OF SMALL FEATHERS
SELECTION OF ITEMS FROM THE
GARDEN – SMALL TWIGS,
PRESSED LEAVES, PRESSED
FERNS, ETC.
SELECTION OF FINE CRAFT
PAPERS, PREFERABLY IN NEUTRAL

AND EARTHY COLOURS
SCISSORS
CRAFT KNIFE
CUTTING MAT
PAGES OF COLOURED NEWSPRINT
(OPTIONAL)
SHEET OF PAPER WITH CHINESE
OR ARABIC SCRIPT (OPTIONAL)
ALL-PURPOSE CRAFT GLUE

1. Choose the focal point of your card – a feather, twig or leaf – and place on a piece of paper to determine the size of the card you will need. Cut out your main card, allowing a border of 2.5–5 cm (1–2") all round the item to be mounted.

2. Take a contrasting piece of paper and cut a square or rectangle just big enough to frame the object you have chosen. Tear the edges slightly for extra effect. Glue the feather/twig/leaf in the middle of the piece of contrasting paper.

3. Alternatively, display the feather by cutting two slits in the contrasting paper and slipping the shaft of the feather through the slits. Use a craft knife and a cutting mat for this.

4. For extra contrast cut yet another piece of card in a third colour, smaller than the main card but larger than the contrasting paper, and stick that down on the main card. You could also add cuttings from newspapers printed on coloured paper or even Arabic or Chinese script, for a really eye-catching effect.

5. To finish, glue the smaller piece of contrasting paper on to the middle of the main card.

2

3

4

Cerne relief cards

Very delicate looking cards and quick to make. Although you can use any colour card you like, I think they work best in soft pastels with the motif outlined in silver paint. Another good one for children to try.

1. Cut out preferred card shape and size.

2. Cut out a piece of textured tissue paper (a little smaller than the front of the card) and tear it to produce a rough edge.

3. Stick the tissue paper on to the card using spray glue (ordinary glue is too heavy for the tissue paper). Leave to dry.

4. Spray the front of the card very lightly with the gold or silver spray paint.

5. Sketch your preferred pattern on to the front of the card in pencil – doves and candles look particularly good.

6. Go over your pencil figure with the outline paint. This might need to be done twice. Allow to dry – it will take about 20 minutes.

MATERIALS:

SELECTION OF CRAFT CARD IN PASTEL SHADES
SCISSORS
TEXTURED OPEN-WEAVE TISSUE PAPER (FROM ART SHOPS)
CAN OF SPRAY GLUE
CAN OF GOLD OR SILVER SPRAY PAINT
PENCIL
TUBE OF CERNE RELIEF OUTLINE PAINT – GOLD OR SILVER (FROM ART SHOPS)

Embossed invitations

These very classy invitations make a change from the run-of-the mill printed ones. But please note that you do need to use an electric hob or iron in the process of making them, so children should be closely supervised.

1. Press the rubber stamp on the ink pad and stamp the design on to the centre of a piece of craft card. Trim the card to size.

2. Sprinkle the card liberally with the silver stamping powder and shake gently to remove any excess.

3. Hold the paper a few inches above an electric hob or an iron on a gentle to medium heat. Use barbecue tongs for this so that you don't burn your fingers. Be very careful not to singe the paper. After a few minutes the powder will melt to form a glossy, slightly raised surface.

4. Leave the card to dry and then write on your message.

MATERIALS:

CRAFT CARD IN YOUR CHOICE OF COLOURS
RUBBER STAMP IN THE DESIGN OF A BORDER (CAN BE BOUGHT OR MADE TO ORDER AT ART SHOPS)
INK PAD
SCISSORS
TUB OF SILVER STAMPING POWDER (FROM ART SHOPS)
PEN

Presents

In the hurried run-up to Christmas, present-buying can become a chore instead of a pleasure, with all thoughts of originality going out the window as we buy almost anything just to be able to cross another name off the list. This is a pity, because giving well-considered presents is as much of a pleasure as receiving them, and homemade presents are often the best of all – chosen with care and made with love.

A really novel way to dress a plain mirror, and very easy to do.

Dried hydrangea
Mirror

MATERIALS:

**MIRROR WITH FLAT FRAME, 5–7 CM (2–3″) WIDE,
PREFERABLY IN WOOD**
BLOCK OF FLORIST'S OASIS
GLUE GUN OR STRONG ALL-PURPOSE GLUE
SELECTION OF DRIED HYDRANGEA HEADS
DRIED ROSE HEADS
ROSE ESSENTIAL OIL

1. Cut the block of oasis into slices about 3.5 cm (1½″) thick and stick them around the edge of the frame – use a glue gun or very strong glue.

2. Cut each of the dried hydrangea heads into approximately 6 florets, and stick the stems firmly into the oasis. Go right round the frame, looking at it from all angles to make sure that there are no gaps.

3. Add a few dried roses for extra impact.

4. Apply a few drops of essential oil to the flower heads if desired for a perfumed finish (opposite).

1

2

3

Decoupage seed box

A simple but effective gift for the avid gardener. Quite often seed packets get thrown into a corner of the shed at the end of the sowing season and then forgotten because there's nowhere suitable to store them. How about making this decorative seed storage box for the gardener in your life? It's also a nice gift for children to make.

1. I used a wooden box for this item, but you could use any plain box, even a metal one.

2. Take the wrapping paper and very carefully cut out the shapes you want to use to decorate the box.

3. Stick the shapes on the box using craft glue.

4. When the glue is dry, seal the surface with several coats of water-based matt varnish. Allow each coat to dry completely before applying the next.

5. If you want to give the box an aged appearance, add a little raw umber acrylic paint to the varnish and it will give it a "yellowed" look. You can even crackle glaze

the lid to give a really antique effect. Crackle glaze, available from art shops, is a clear varnish that you simply paint on, and when it dries it creates a "crackled" mottled effect.

> **MATERIALS:**
>
> PLAIN BOX, LARGE ENOUGH TO HOLD PACKETS OF SEEDS
> WRAPPING PAPER PRINTED WITH FRUIT AND VEGETABLE MOTIFS
> SCISSORS
> ALL-PURPOSE CRAFT GLUE
> TIN OF WATER-BASED MATT VARNISH
> TUBE OF RAW UMBER ACRYLIC PAINT
> TWO 2.5 CM (1″) PAINTBRUSHES

Gardener's skincare kit

How about this as a gift inspired by the garden – a skincare kit for the person who spends a lot of time working out in the open. First, an invigorating homemade footbath, perfect for tired toes. Peppermint has long been valued for its antiseptic and cooling properties.

Homemade peppermint footbath

1. Take several stems of fresh peppermint or dried peppermint leaves and place in the saucepan with the juniper berries. Add 720 ml (1¼pt) water and heat slowly to just below boiling point, stirring once in a while. Cover the saucepan and leave to cool.

2. While the mixture is still warm, add 6 drops each of sandalwood and cypress essential oil and stir well.

3. Use a funnel and strain the liquid through a coffee filter paper into a decorative jar. Seal and label.

4. To use the footbath, fill a bowl with warm/hot water, pour in a cup of the peppermint mixture and soak the feet for ten minutes.

> **MATERIALS:**
>
> STEMS OF FRESH PEPPERMINT OR DRIED PEPPERMINT LEAVES
> 100 G (4 OZ) JUNIPER BERRIES
> NON-ALUMINIUM SAUCEPAN
> SANDALWOOD ESSENTIAL OIL
> CYPRESS ESSENTIAL OIL
> FUNNEL AND COFFEE FILTER PAPER
> DECORATIVE JAR WITH TIGHT-FITTING LID

Rose moisturiser

A beautiful handcream that will be thoroughly appreciated by the hardworking gardener.

1. Put the beeswax and lanolin in the small mixing bowl. Melt this over a saucepan of hot water on a low heat.

2. Add 3 tablespoons of almond oil and beat together. Put the mixing bowl in a warm place.

3. Using a clean, non-aluminium saucepan, heat the rosewater and a pinch of borax to about 50°C (122°F) and add slowly to the mixing bowl, whisking the mixture together. Stand the bowl in a larger bowl of cold water and continue whisking until the cream is cold.

4. Spoon the cream into a decorative jar and label.

> **MATERIALS:**
>
> 1 TSP BEESWAX (OR USE A CHUNK OF BEESWAX CANDLE)
> 3 TSP LANOLIN (FROM CHEMIST'S SHOP)
> SMALL MIXING BOWL
> ALMOND OIL (FROM CHEMIST)
> NON-ALUMINIUM SAUCEPAN
> 125 ML (¼PT) ROSEWATER (FROM CHEMIST)
> BORAX (FROM CHEMIST)
> LARGE MIXING BOWL
> WHISK
> DECORATIVE JAR

Winter bark bulb holder

A great way to decorate an otherwise dull indoor plant holder, so that it is an object of beauty even before the bulb bursts into flower.

1. Break up some pieces of bark and glue them around the pot, making sure that they cover all the terracotta.

2. Fill any gaps by gluing on the moss and seed heads.

3. Decorate the pot with a raffia bow.

4. Plant the bulb in the pot and cover the compost with moss.

MATERIALS:

PLAIN TERRACOTTA PLANT POT
LARGE PIECES OF BARK
WOOD GLUE
MOSS
SEED HEADS (FROM FLORIST'S SHOPS)
RAFFIA OR WIDE HESSIAN RIBBON
BULB AND COMPOST

Homemade chutney

There is nothing quite like homemade chutney with cheese and crusty bread, and this chutney will go down a treat as a gift.

INGREDIENTS (MAKES 4 LB CHUTNEY):
200 G (8 OZ) BRAMLEY APPLES, FINELY CUBED
200 G (8 OZ) BLOCK DATES
200 G (8 OZ) SULTANAS
200 G (8 OZ) RED ONIONS, FINELY CHOPPED
200 G (8 OZ) SOFT BROWN SUGAR
1 TSP SALT
¼ TSP ENGLISH MUSTARD POWDER
¼ TSP CHILLI POWDER
275 ML (½ PT) SPICED VINEGAR

1. Finely chop all the ingredients and mix thoroughly with the sugar, salt and spices.

2. Pour on the vinegar, mix thoroughly and leave to stand until the sugar has dissolved.

3. Bottle in sterilised jars. Keep cool. Serve with ham, stilton or cheddar cheese.

Gilded candles

The fine tracery on these candles gives them a wonderfully delicate quality and they make beautiful but inexpensive gifts.

1. Cover your work surface with newspaper.

2. Rest the candle on the newspaper and hold it by the wick so that it is leaning at an angle. Then with as steady a hand as possible, draw patterns all round the candle with the relief paint. You can be as detailed as you like – lace-like patterns look especially good.

3. Leave to dry for about 20 minutes.
   NB: The cerne relief paint will melt as the candle does.

MATERIALS:

CHURCH CANDLES OF YOUR CHOICE
TUBES OF CERNE RELIEF PAINT IN SILVER, BRONZE OR GOLD (FROM ART SHOPS)
NEWSPAPER

Scented room spray

This is a wonderfully subtle alternative to harshly perfumed commercial room sprays. Pour it into an old-fashioned bottle to create a really elegant present.

MATERIALS:

10 ML (⅓ FL OZ) METHYLATED SPIRITS
15 DROPS CHAMOMILE ESSENTIAL OIL
15 DROPS JASMINE ESSENTIAL OIL
10 DROPS LAVENDER ESSENTIAL OIL
45 DROPS BERGAMOT ESSENTIAL OIL
500 ML (17 FL OZ) DISTILLED WATER (FROM CHEMIST)
DECORATIVE PUMP-ACTION SPRAY BOTTLE

1. Pour the methylated spirits into a small bowl and add the oils. Mix well.

2. Pour the distilled water into the spray bottle and add the oil mixture.

3. Replace the lid and shake well.

Gift Wrapping

When I was little my parents used to forbid us to go into the "Christmas" room until Christmas Eve. Needless to say, we always used to sneak in when they weren't around and try to work out what all the lovely packages contained. Half the fun was in the looking and guessing, and inventive wrapping makes the whole build-up to the big moment all the more exciting.

Drummer boy box

This is really stunning and makes a great toy when it has served its purpose as a gift wrapping.

1. Paint the outside of the box and the lid in the bright red emulsion paint.

2. Cut a strip of cardboard the same depth as the lid and glue it around the bottom of the box with PVA glue. Paint this too.

3. Using the bradawl or any sharp, pointed tool, make a row of widely spaced holes on the side of the box just above the glued-on cardboard, and another row just below the top of the box, so that when you thread your string it will form a diagonal pattern. Push brass paper fasteners through these holes, leaving 2 holes empty at opposite sides of the box. Do not fix the paper fasteners too tightly.

4. Take a long length of gold string and wind it around each paper fastener, following the diagonal pattern you have established. If necessary, tighten the paper fasteners to hold the string in place.

5. Take some gold braid or fringing and glue it around the rim of the lid and the cardboard strip at the bottom of the box.

6. Thread a length of gold cord through the 2 remaining holes in the side of the box and tie a knot at each end inside the box, forming a handle.

7. To make the drumsticks, spray the small polystyrene balls with the gold paint. Then take the pencils, or 2 pencil-length sticks of wood, and push one ball on to each of them. Use PVA glue to secure the balls on the sticks – clear glue will dissolve the balls. Glue the drumsticks to the top of the box.

8. Line the inside of the box with a strip of fancy paper, to cover the back of the fasteners.

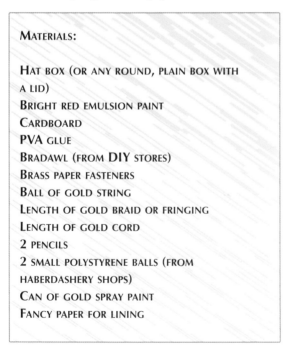

MATERIALS:

HAT BOX (OR ANY ROUND, PLAIN BOX WITH A LID)
BRIGHT RED EMULSION PAINT
CARDBOARD
PVA GLUE
BRADAWL (FROM DIY STORES)
BRASS PAPER FASTENERS
BALL OF GOLD STRING
LENGTH OF GOLD BRAID OR FRINGING
LENGTH OF GOLD CORD
2 PENCILS
2 SMALL POLYSTYRENE BALLS (FROM HABERDASHERY SHOPS)
CAN OF GOLD SPRAY PAINT
FANCY PAPER FOR LINING

Pine cone gift basket

Very seasonal and an enchanting way to present homemade food or beauty preparations.

1. Take the mixing bowl and measure underneath from side to side. Add 10 cm (4 inches) to this measurement.

2. Cut a circular paper template using the above measurement as the diameter then, using gloves, cut out a circle of soft chicken wire around the template.

3. Mould the wire around the bowl, leaving the piece that will go over the lip so you can release and remove the bowl.

4. Fold over and firm up the lip of the basket, then take a strip of chicken wire and fashion a handle for the basket.

5. Using florist's wire, attach the pine cones to the basket until the outside of the basket is covered. (Wire the pine cones by pulling the wire tightly around the inside of the top layer of "petals", at the flat end of the cone.

> **MATERIALS:**
>
> **MEDIUM MIXING BOWL – PREFERABLY PLASTIC**
> **FLEXIBLE TAPE MEASURE**
> **LARGE PIECE OF PAPER**
> **PAIR OF GLOVES**
> **LARGE PIECE OF CHICKEN WIRE**
> **PLIERS**
> **LARGE SELECTION OF MEDIUM SIZED PINE CONES**
> **(DRIED OVERNIGHT OR IN THE MICROWAVE)**
> **FLORIST'S WIRES**
> **BALL OF RUSTIC STRING**
> **BAG OF DRIED FLORIST'S MOSS**
> **FAKE BIRDS (OPTIONAL)**

6. Wind some string around the handle until it is completely covered. Using florist's wire, attach the handle to the inside of the basket.

7. Fill in the gaps between the cones with dried moss and then line the basket with moss. Finish off with fake birds around the rim of the basket, if desired.

Gilded tags

Christmas wouldn't be Christmas without a bit of gold somewhere! So protect your work surface with newspaper and have some fun splashing a bit of paint around.

1. Work in a well-ventilated room – the fumes from the paint can be quite strong.

2. Lay the cards out on the newspaper and, wearing the gloves, use the sponge and brushes to decorate them with the paint. Experiment with dragging, splattering and sponging. The secret is not to put too much paint on the brush or sponge. Leave to dry.

3. Punch a hole in the corner of each card, write your message on the other side and attach the card to your present with gold thread.

> **MATERIALS:**
>
> **CRAFT CARD OF YOUR CHOICE, CUT TO GIFT TAG SIZE**
> **POT OF GOLD OR BRONZE PAINT (FROM ART SHOPS)**
> **NEWSPAPER**
> **RUBBER GLOVES**
> **SELECTION OF SMALL PAINTBRUSHES**
> **SMALL SPONGE**
> **HOLE PUNCH**
> **GOLD THREAD**

Fancy dress wrapping

A really wacky way to present a gift – dressed in its own tuxedo!

1. Using double-sided sticky tape, stick a piece of white paper on the front of the shoebox.

2. Cut a piece of black paper the same height as the box and wide enough to go right round it. Stick it to the box so that the open ends meet in the middle of the front of the box. Fold down the top corners at a slant to imitate jacket lapels.

3. Stick sequins down the front of the white "shirt" as buttons.

4. Cut a bow tie and triangular handkerchief from the red card and stick in place.

5. Finish off the bow tie with sequins.

> **MATERIALS:**
>
> CARDBOARD SHOEBOX
> SHEET OF WHITE PAPER
> SHEET OF BLACK ART PAPER
> SCISSORS
> DOUBLE-SIDED STICKY TAPE
> ALL-PURPOSE CLEAR ADHESIVE
> SEQUINS
> SHEET OF RED CARD

Parchment paper

All it takes is a humble teabag to produce very authentic-looking parchment paper. This is an inexpensive but effective idea.

1. Squeeze the damp teabags to remove any excess water.

2. Lay out a sheet of the lining paper and rub a teabag over it. Don't worry if it looks a little streaky. Leave to dry.

3. If you want to intensify the colour, repeat the process and leave to dry again.

4. When the paper is absolutely dry it will wrinkle slightly and take on a browned parchment effect.

5. Complement the parchment wrapping by using a wax seal and red ribbon to dress the present.

> **MATERIALS:**
>
> ROLL OF WHITE OR CREAM LINING PAPER (FROM DECORATING SHOPS)
> DAMP TEABAGS
> DECORATIVE SEAL (FROM MOST STATIONERS) OR AN EMBOSSED RING FROM YOUR JEWELLERY BOX
> SEALING WAX
> FANCY RIBBON

Paste grain paper

A fun idea for children to try. The secret is not to put too much paste on the paper, or else it will become wrinkled.

1. Mix up some wallpaper paste in the bowl, following the packet instructions for the thicker version of the paste.

2. Mix in your choice of paint until you achieve the desired colour.

3. Brush the paint mixture quite roughly on to the lining paper.

4. Use the cardboard comb to drag patterns through the wet paint/paste mixture. Alternatively, use printing blocks to imprint the pattern of your choice. Leave to dry.

MATERIALS:

OLD BOWL AND SPOON
WALLPAPER PASTE (BUY CHILD-FRIENDLY VERSION)
SAMPLE POTS OF EMULSION PAINT
WIDE PAINTBRUSH
ROLL OF LINING PAPER (FROM DECORATING SHOPS)
A PIECE OF THICK CARD, CUT INTO A COMB SHAPE, OR A PRINTING BLOCK OF YOUR CHOICE

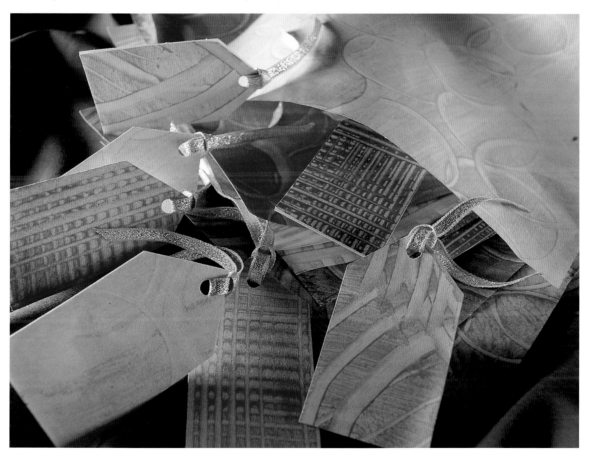

Wreaths and Garlands

I always think that wreaths and garlands represent the more elegant side of Christmas. This chapter contains some really lovely variations on the theme which would grace any home and are a delightful respite from the paper chains I remember from years gone past. The nut swag is particularly effective and will last for many years.

Nut swag

A very elegant and natural-looking Christmas decoration. This nut swag can be made to any length, but it can become quite heavy, so ensure that you provide adequate support when hanging it.

1. Spray the toilet rolls with the bronze paint and leave to dry.

2. Using the glue gun, stick the nuts all over the toilet rolls, building them up one on top of the other until the cardboard can no longer be seen.

3. Cover as many toilet rolls as you need to create the desired length of swag.

4. Varnish the nuts and leave them to dry completely. The varnish will heighten their colour and create a much more professional finish.

5. Thread the toilet rolls on to the rope and hang where desired. You will find that the swag is very flexible because it is made in so many sections.

6. For added decoration, twist lengths of real ivy around the toilet rolls. Remember that ivy is poisonous!

MATERIALS:

TOILET ROLLS OR CARDBOARD POSTER TUBES CUT INTO TOILET-ROLL SIZED PIECES
BRONZE SPRAY PAINT
LARGE QUANTITY OF ASSORTED NUTS IN THEIR SHELLS
GLUE GUN
TIN OF POLYURETHANE VARNISH AND SMALL PAINTBRUSH
LONG PIECE OF THIN ROPE

Bronzed ivy circlet

A simple but effective wreath which looks as if it's made from metal leaves.

1. Work the branches of ivy into a round and secure with the wire so that you have a neat circlet.

2. Place the circlet on newspaper and spray liberally with bronze spray paint. Leave to dry.

3. Repeat the process until the ivy is completely covered with bronze paint and looks like metal.

MATERIALS:

SEVERAL BRANCHES OF FRESH IVY
SOME FLORIST'S WIRE
BRONZE SPRAY PAINT
SHEETS OF NEWSPAPER

4. Hang the circlet from a ribbon.

Cabbage and hydrangea head wreath

An unusual combination, but I love the colours and textures of this wall wreath. You can just remove the cabbages when they lose their freshness, and keep the dried hydrangea framework for another occasion.

1. Cut a strip of chicken wire, about 25 cm (10") wide and as long as you want the wreath to be.

2. Lay a good amount of moss in the centre of the strip and fold round the chicken wire to create a sausage. Secure with florist's wires. You may want to wear gloves for this.

3. Attach the ends of the chicken wire together with more wire so that you have a circular wreath.

4. Peel back the outer layers of the cabbages so that they look like the petals of a flower. Use the florist's wires to attach the cabbages to the wreath. The cabbages will be relatively heavy so you'll need to put 2 or 3 wires in each one and use a bradawl to make the holes for the wires.

MATERIALS:

LARGE PIECE OF CHICKEN WIRE
LARGE BAG OF FLORIST'S MOSS
PLIERS
PAIR OF GLOVES
FLORIST'S WIRES
BRADAWL
SEVERAL SMALL SAVOY CABBAGES
DRIED HYDRANGEA HEADS
BAG OF BRUSSELS SPROUTS
STRONG WIRED RIBBON OR ROPE

5. Fill in the gaps between the cabbages with hydrangea heads and bunches of wired Brussels sprouts – again, using florist's wires.

6. Attach a loop made of ribbon or rope and hang up your wreath.

Lemon and lime *Wreath*

Fragrance and colour in one – a really eye-catching wall or table wreath.

MATERIALS:

FLORIST'S OASIS RING WITH PLASTIC BACKING
(FROM FLORIST'S SHOP)
LARGE BUNCH OF 30 CM (12") FLORIST'S WIRES
SELECTION OF VARIEGATED IVY LEAVES
LARGE SELECTION OF SMALL LEMONS AND LIMES
BOX OF KUMQUATS
ORNAMENTAL FOLIAGE FROM THE GARDEN

1. Soak the oasis ring in water.

2. Wire some small bunches of ivy leaves all round the oasis.

3. Feed 2 florist's wires through the bottom half of each lemon and lime and wind these around the oasis, securing firmly. You want to cover as much of the oasis with fruit as possible, bearing in mind that the finished wreath should not be too heavy.

4. Wire on the kumquats to disguise any gaps.

5. Finish by wiring more ivy into the oasis ring to cover up any remaining bare wires.

2

3

4

Copper leaf garland

A shimmering fantasy, this wreath looks at its best when hung above a fireplace, so that the copper metal leaves can catch the glow from the fire.

1. Using a paper template if necessary, cut leaf shapes about 7.5–10 cm (3–4") long from the copper foil – oak and ivy both work well. Include a thin 2.5 cm (1") stem on each leaf. You might find it more comfortable to wear gloves for this. If the edges of the foil are too sharp, smooth them off with emery paper or a metal file.

2. Cut the copper picture hanging wire to the same length as the desired length of your garland.

3. Attach the leaves to the wire, winding the stems round the wire. Space them close together, to achieve a bunched effect. Keep going until you have covered the whole length of the wire. If necessary, use a glue gun to fix the leaves in place.

> **MATERIALS:**
>
> ROLL OF COPPER FOIL (FROM CRAFT SHOPS AND BY MAIL ORDER)
> TIN SNIPPERS (FROM BUILDERS MERCHANTS)
> GLOVES
> METAL FILE OR EMERY PAPER
> ROLL OF COPPER PICTURE HANGING WIRE
> GLUE GUN

4. The finished garland looks spectacular fixed to a dark beam or fireplace mantle. Being made of metal, the garland will last forever, but you may have to polish it up once in a while to preserve the beautiful copper lustre.

Star wreath

This is the sort of decoration you would see in Germany at Christmas time. Please note that it is meant purely for ornamentation and is not to be eaten.

1. Mix the flour, salt, chocolate powder and water and knead well, adding more flour or water as needed.

2. Roll the dough until it is approximately 6 mm (¼") thick and cut out star shapes with the cutter.

3. Lay the star shapes in a circle on the baking sheet, each one overlapping the next.

4. Bake at 150°C/ 300°F/ Gas Mark 2 for 1 hour.

5. Leave to cool.

6. Varnish the whole wreath and leave to dry completely.

7. Hang the wreath from a ribbon.

INGREDIENTS:

2 LEVEL MUGS PLAIN FLOUR
1 MUG SALT
4 TBSP CHOCOLATE POWDER
350 ML (12 FL OZ) LUKEWARM WATER
EXTRA FLOUR AND WATER
ROLLING PIN
STAR CUTTER
BAKING SHEET
TIN OF POLYURETHANE VARNISH
SMALL PAINTBRUSH
RIBBON

Pine cone wreath

A wreath which highlights the beauty of nature and needs no special adornment.

1. Wire a selection of pine cones by slipping one end of a florist's wire under the top row of scales on each cone (at the flatter end of the cone) and securing tightly.

2. Taking the larger cones first, wire them all round the wreath, with the open cone pointing always to the outside.

3. Using the secateurs, cut some of the medium sized cones in half, creating what looks like an open flower head.

4. Wire these "flowers" on to the front of the wreath.

5. Fill in any remaining spaces with smaller cones, using the glue gun if necessary.

6. Hang the wreath from a ribbon.

MATERIALS:

FLORIST'S WIRE
ASSORTMENT OF PINE CONES – DRY AND OPENED OUT
WILLOW FLORIST'S WREATH
PAIR OF SECATEURS
GLUE GUN
RIBBON

Room Decorations

The home takes on a special significance at Christmas. It's where we spend time with family and loved ones, where we welcome guests and hold parties, and where we seek some quiet time to reflect upon the past year. The house is probably never under such scrutiny as it is at Christmas, and a few well-chosen decorations can have great impact. The secret is to choose a single decorative theme, and not to have too many different items competing with one other.

Citrus fruit pomanders

One of the simplest and most effective ideas I have seen – a lovely way both to decorate and perfume the room.

1. Take one fruit at a time, hold the sharp end of the cutter away from your body and parallel to the surface of the fruit, and cut patterns into the skin of the fruit. Geometric patterns and swirls look particularly good. Only go as far down as the pith. Don't dig into the wet part of the fruit or it will go bad.

2. Let the fruit dry in a cool place – it will take a few days. Don't try to dry the fruit in the oven as it will shrivel and lose its shape.

3. For extra protection, give the fruit a coating of clear varnish.

4. Pile the fruit high on the cake stand. It will look fabulous.

MATERIALS:

ORANGES, LEMONS AND LIMES
FINE LINO CUTTING TOOL (FROM ART SHOPS)
TIN OF CLEAR VARNISH
SMALL PAINTBRUSH
ORNATE CAKE STAND

Christmas tree wall wreath

A fun variation on the freestanding Christmas tree. You can make any size wall wreath but for this version, which is about 60 cm (24") high, you need the following:

1. Fasten bamboo canes together in a triangular shape using string or wire.

2. Cut out 2 triangles of chicken wire, slightly larger than the triangle of bamboo and secure with florist's wire to the bamboo frame, one piece either side, leaving the wide bottom end open.

3. Wearing gardening gloves, feed the moss into the wire cage, packing quite tightly and pushing it up to the top with another cane if necessary.

4. Fix the greenery of your choice to the outside by feeding it into the holes of the chicken wire, which will hold it in place quite easily. The aim is to imitate the branches of a tree.

5. Decorate with fruit attached to florist's wire, or whatever you prefer.

MATERIALS:

2 BAMBOO CANES EACH 80 CM (32") LONG
1 BAMBOO CANE 62 CM (25") LONG
STRING OR WIRE
1.4 M (1½ YARDS) OF 75 CM (30") CHICKEN WIRE
FLORIST'S WIRE
GARDENING GLOVES
LARGE QUANTITY OF MOSS
STRING
BRANCHES FROM AN EVERGREEN TREE
FRUIT, TRADITIONAL TREE BAUBLES AND WHITE
FAIRY LIGHTS (OPTIONAL)

6. As an extra, feed a string of white fairy lights through the back of the tree. When hanging the tree, remember to plug the lights in first, then you'll know how much flex you have to play with and where you can put the tree!

Illustrated opposite

Star fruit flower decoration

A really novel way of presenting flowers in a vase – and it takes just minutes to put together.

1. Place the jam jar in the bowl and secure it in place by packing moss all around it.

2. Slide slices of the star fruit in between the moss and the glass – the green of the moss will highlight the yellow of the star fruit brilliantly.

3. Fill the jam jar and with water and arrange your flowers as desired – orange flowers blend well with the star fruit.

MATERIALS:

LARGE ROUND BOWL – A GOLDFISH BOWL IS IDEAL
JAM JAR, NO TALLER THAN THE ROUND BOWL
BAG OF FLORIST'S MOSS
3 STAR FRUITS (FROM MOST SUPERMARKETS)
SELECTION OF FLOWERS IN ORANGE, YELLOW AND RED

Marzipan Tree

A real conversation piece – a miniature tree shimmering with edible marzipan fruits. Please note that the fruits are secured to the tree with florist's wire, which must of course be removed before the marzipan is eaten.

MATERIALS:

TERRACOTTA FLOWER POT 20 CM (8") HIGH
CAN OF SILVER SPRAY PAINT
TREE BRANCH APPROXIMATELY 37–45 CM
(15–18") HIGH, WITH EVENLY SPLAYED
OFFSHOOTS AND LEAVES REMOVED
SELECTION OF SMALL PEBBLES
BLOCK OF FLORIST'S OASIS
HANDFUL OF MOSS
ALUMINIUM FOIL
COCKTAIL STICKS
SCISSORS
BLOCK OF MARZIPAN
SELECTION OF FOOD COLOURINGS
TUB OF EDIBLE SILVER DUSTING POWDER
GREEN PLASTIC-COVERED FLORIST'S WIRE, WHICH
MUST BE ABSOLUTELY CLEAN
PAIR OF PLIERS

1. Spray the pot silver and leave to dry. Stand the branch in the pot and secure in place with the pebbles, using slithers of the oasis to pack the branch in really tightly. Lay moss around the base of the tree to disguise the oasis.

2. Cut small leaves 2.5–5 cm (1–2") from the aluminium foil, making sure that they have a stem about 2.5 cm (1") long. Use a cocktail stick to impress veins on the leaf. Attach the leaves to the tree by winding the stem around the branches.

3. Take small lumps of marzipan and colour with food colouring. Fashion into fruit shapes and rub the fruits with edible silver dusting powder until they take on a silver sheen.

4. Thread a piece of florist's wire through each fruit, cut the wire to the desired length, form a hook at both ends, push one end into the fruit and hang from the tree.

Glazed nut table coronet

This is one of my favourite creations. It's simple to make, looks elegant, lasts forever and has a multitude of uses – as a wall wreath, table centrepiece, Advent wreath or harvest festival decoration.

1. Using the glue gun, take the larger nuts and glue them all around the sides and top of the wreath, building one on top of another.

2. Fill in any gaps with the smaller nuts, so that the wreath is completely covered with nuts. Leave to dry.

3. Do not glue nuts to the underside of the wreath, as this will prevent it sitting or hanging comfortably.

4. Give the nuts a coat of varnish. This will enhance their natural beauty and strengthen the wreath.

MATERIALS:

FLORIST'S WREATH, PREFERABLY MADE OF WILLOW
OR SOME OTHER NATURAL MATERIAL
GLUE GUN
LARGE ASSORTMENT OF NUTS WITH
  THEIR SHELLS ON
TIN OF POLYURETHANE VARNISH
SMALL PAINTBRUSH

5. Add any extra decoration you like – a bow or some Advent candles to sit in the middle of the wreath.

Ice ball lanterns

I have a favourite idea for every season, and this is my winter blockbuster. These ice ball lanterns are a real wow and will be the talking point of any party – for maximum effect make them in pairs to stand at the front door or gate.

1. Fill the balloon with water and tie a knot at the top.

2. Put the bucket with the balloon inside in the freezer for several hours or until about 1.5 cm (½ ") ice has formed all around the inside of the balloon.

3. Take the bucket out of the freezer and cut the balloon away from the ice ball.

4. Use a serrated knife or small saw to cut a lid off the top of the ice ball.

5. Pour out the water and scrape out any soft ice left in the centre of the ice ball.

MATERIALS:

ONE BALLOON PER LANTERN
ONE BUCKET PER LANTERN
SMALL SAW OR SERRATED KNIFE
SEVERAL VOTIVE CANDLES
PAIR OF BARBECUE TONGS

6. Put the ice ball back in the bucket . Replace in the freezer until you are ready to use it.

7. When appropriate, position the lanterns outdoors and put the votive candle inside the lantern – a pair of barbecue tongs would be helpful for this.

Fresh flower wall sconce

We tend to forget fresh flowers at Christmas, but they really are a breath of fresh air amidst all the tinsel.

1. Place the oasis on the plastic plate. Trim off any overhanging edges with a knife (it might set your teeth on edge a little!)

2. Sit the plate on the sheet of chicken wire and, wearing gardening gloves, wrap the wire around the plate and oasis. Use the pliers to cut off any protruding wire and secure if necessary with florist's wires.

3. Dampen the oasis and decorate with your favourite flowers. They will sit quite securely in the oasis with the added support of the chicken wire. Make use of ivy and grasses to increase the spread of the arrangement.

4. Attach a ribbon loop to the chicken wire and hang on the wall. These arrangements look particularly effective hung from wall sconces.

MATERIALS:

PLASTIC PLATE
BLOCK OF FLORIST'S OASIS (WET VARIETY)
KNIFE
LARGE PIECE OF CHICKEN WIRE
PAIR OF GARDENING GLOVES
FLORIST'S WIRES
PLIERS
SELECTION OF FRESH FLOWERS, IVY, GRASSES
RIBBON

The plastic plate will protect the wall from any damp.

5. Remember to refresh the oasis with a little water from time to time.

Tree
Decorations

L egend has it that Martin Luther started the tradition of decorating the Christmas tree, to symbolise the starry sky from where Jesus came. What I like about tree decorating is the chance to create really detailed items – little slippers, bejewelled baubles and richly decorated fabric shapes. Admittedly, these things do take that bit longer to make, but they have a permanence that many of the trappings of Christmas lack, and some may even become family heirlooms.

Kasbah Slippers

These are real fairy slippers – tiny, sparkling and mysterious. I can just imagine the elves working through the night to have them finished in time for Christmas.

1. Cut a slipper template out of card, about 7.5 cm (3") long and 4 cm (1 ½") wide and make as many copies as you want slippers. Glue a felt square on to one side of each slipper template and cut out. Cut another piece of felt the same size and set aside. Decorate around the edge of the glued felt with a fine braid, leaving the toe of the slipper bare.

2. Glue a loop of thread on the uncovered side of the card.

3. Cut an oval piece of metallic crepe paper, the width of which should be the same as the distance from the toe to the middle of the slipper. You can use velvet or other fabric, but metallic crepe paper is good because it is malleable and doesn't fray, which is very helpful during the next step.

4. Mould the metallic crepe paper or fabric round the template to make the upper of the shoe and glue it at the back. If using the metallic crepe paper, cut fancy shapes into the raw edge of the upper to make it look

more finished.

5. Stick the other piece of felt on the back and decorate the front of the slipper with fake gemstones – the more elaborate the better.

MATERIALS:

SHEET OF THIN CARD
PENCIL AND SCISSORS
SQUARES OF FELT IN DIFFERENT COLOURS
FABRIC GLUE
SELECTION OF NARROW BRAIDS
COLOURED THREAD
METALLIC CREPE PAPER (OR VELVET OR OTHER FABRIC)
SELECTION OF FAKE GEMSTONES (FROM HABERDASHERS)

1
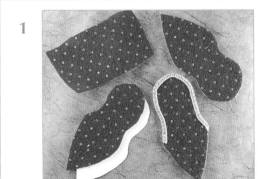

2
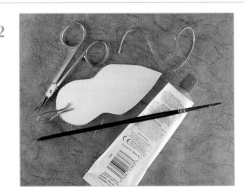

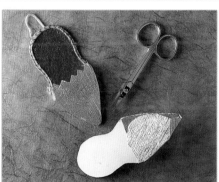

4

5

Renaissance hand-marbled baubles

Reminiscent of Venetian glass, these decorations are quite exquisite and great fun to make.

1. Half-fill the bowl with warm water. The paint will be very difficult to remove, so don't use your favourite bowl.

2. Wearing the rubber gloves, shake the paints well and drizzle a teaspoon of whichever colours you want into the bowl of water. Silver and red go well together, as do blue and green, but the choice is yours. The more colours you use, the greater the kaleidoscope effect you will create.

3. If the colours move to the side of the bowl, give it a quick stir so that the paint swirls round the bowl.

4. Dip the baubles quickly into the paint mixture. If you want a more striking result, dip them several times.

MATERIALS:

OLD PLASTIC BOWL
RUBBER GLOVES
VARIETY OF NON WATER-SOLUBLE CERAMIC PAINTS
OLD WOODEN SPOON
SEVERAL PLAIN GLASS BAUBLES – FROSTED OR MATT, NOT SHINY
COLOURED RIBBON

5. Hang the baubles up to dry.

6. Finish by tying small bows of coloured ribbon around the top of the bauble if desired.

Wonderful wire baubles

A contemporary twist on the traditional tree bauble and very suitable for a modern or minimalist interior.

1. Take the tops off the baubles.

2. Cut lengths of wire and feed the wire into the baubles. It will take on interesting shapes as it moulds itself to the inside of the baubles.

3. Replace the metal pin tops.

4. Alternatively, wind the wire round a pencil to create a corkscrew effect and then feed this into the baubles, or wind the wire around the outside of the bauble – attach one end to the metal pin top and then gently scrunch the wire

MATERIALS:

CLEAR GLASS OR PLASTIC BAUBLES WITH
REMOVABLE METAL PIN TOPS
COPPER, ALUMINIUM OR BRONZE CRAFT WIRE
(FROM HABERDASHERY DEPARTMENTS)
PLIERS
PENCIL

all round the bauble, being careful not to crack the bauble by applying too much pressure!

Salt dough camels

Salt dough camels look like old-fashioned decorations made from wood, but are actually made from the same type of dough I used for the Star Wreath (see page 37). Please note that they are for decoration only and not for eating.

1. Mix the flour and salt with the water and knead well, adding more flour or water as required.

2. Roll out to approximately 6 mm (¼") thick and cut out camel shapes with a pastry cutter (or you could use any other shape you liked). This quantity makes about 50 camels.

3. Mark the outline of the reins and saddle with the knitting needle and make a hole in the back to hang the camel by.

4. Put the camels on a baking tray and bake for 1 hour at 150°C/ 300°F/ Gas Mark 2. Leave to cool.

5. Decorate the camels by gluing on coloured thread for their reins and using the acrylic paints to colour their saddles, manes, etc.

6. Finish off with a coat of polyurethane varnish for extra protection.

MATERIALS:

2 LEVEL MUGS PLAIN FLOUR
1 MUG SALT
350 ML (12 FL OZ) LUKEWARM WATER
EXTRA FLOUR AND WATER
ROLLING PIN
CAMEL-SHAPED PASTRY CUTTER
THIN KNITTING NEEDLE
BAKING SHEET
COLOURED THREAD
FABRIC GLUE
ACRYLIC PAINTS
SMALL GOLD BEADS
TIN OF POLYURETHANE VARNISH (OR ANY GOOD
ARTIST'S VARNISH)
GOLD THREAD
SMALL PAINTBRUSHES

7. Thread the camels and hang them from the tree.

Snowflakes

As delicate as lace, these snowflake decorations are not only beautiful but will last quite a long time because of the protective coating of varnish. Please note that they are not to be eaten – however much they may look like biscuits!

1. Make and bake the snowflakes according to the recipe for the salt dough camels (see p.51), but using a star cutter instead of a camel cutter. Before baking, use a knitting needle to make a hole at the edge of each star.

2. When cooked, allow the stars to cool completely.

3. Pipe cobweb patterns on to the stars with royal icing to create the "lace-like" appearance of a snowflake. Whilst the icing is still tacky, decorate further with silver cake balls.

4. Cover the whole "snowflake", back and front, with a coat of polyurethane varnish – this will prevent the salt dough from going soggy.

5. Put silver thread through the hole for hanging.

INGREDIENTS:
2 LEVEL MUGS PLAIN FLOUR
1 MUG SALT
350 ML (12 FL OZ) LUKEWARM WATER
EXTRA FLOUR AND WATER
ROLLING PIN
STAR-SHAPED PASTRY CUTTER
KNITTING NEEDLE
BAKING SHEET
PIPING BAG WITH FINE NOZZLE FILLED WITH ROYAL ICING
SILVER CAKE DECORATING BALLS (FROM SUPERMARKETS)
TIN OF POLYURETHANE VARNISH
SMALL PAINTBRUSH
SILVER THREAD

Fabric baubles

Really elegant tree decorations that aren't nearly as difficult to make as they may appear.

1. Cut a strip of fabric 7.5 cm (3") wide and long enough to cover the whole bauble.

2. Spray the fabric with fabric stiffener.

3. Wrap the fabric around the bauble, scrunching it as you go. It will stick easily to the bauble because of the stiffener. Leave to dry overnight.

4. Spray with metallic paint and leave to dry.

5. Finish off by rubbing parts of the bauble with gilt cream to highlight it.

MATERIALS:

SELECTION OF PLASTIC OR POLYSTYRENE BAUBLES
FLIMSY COTTON FABRIC IN RICH COLOURS
CAN OF FABRIC STIFFENER
TINS OF GOLD, SILVER AND BRONZE SPRAY PAINT
GILT CREAM (FROM ART SHOPS)

Velvet and pearl drops

Inspired by the bejewelled "cobweb" hairnets that Renaissance women used to wear, these sumptuous pearl-encrusted drops do take a little longer to make than some of my ideas, but they will last for many years and are quite lovely.

1. Fold the fabric, right sides together, and cut out whatever shapes you fancy – stars, circles, hearts. Make the shapes at least 7.5 cm (3") wide.

2. Stitch round the edge, right sides still together, leaving a gap of about 5 cm (2") unsewn.

3. Turn the shapes inside out so that the right side of the fabric is on the outside.

4. Stuff the shapes with wadding and sew up the gap.

5. Take some gold or silver thread and decorate the shapes with a simple stitch such as chainstitch. The aim is to try and create a

MATERIALS:

LENGTH OF VELVET, PREFERABLY DARK RED OR DARK BLUE
WADDING OR ANY AVAILABLE LIGHT STUFFING
SCISSORS
LARGE NEEDLE
PLAIN DARK THREAD AND GOLD OR SILVER THREAD
FAKE PEARL BEADS

lattice-work effect with the thread – be as detailed as possible.

6. Finish the decoration by sewing on fake pearls.

Table
Decorations

Probably my favourite aspect of Christmas decorating, the table setting is a chance to be as theatrical and whimsical as you dare. There are very few opportunities like the grand finale of a Christmas lunch to indulge your decorating fantasies. So if you are going to put extra effort in anywhere at Christmas, it should perhaps be here, at the festive table.

"Tree of Life" place names

These enchanting place name cards never fail to draw admiring comments.

1. Cut a 7.5 cm (3") square piece of card and fold it in half.

2. Pierce a small hole in the middle of the fold.

3. Thread 8 beads on to a 7.5 cm (3") strand of wire. Repeat this until you have 8 strands of wire.

4. Tie a knot at one end of each strand to stop the beads coming off.

5. Take a pair of beaded strands and form a Y figure by intertwining the 2 as yet unbeaded sections of wire.

6. Thread another 8 beads on to this intertwined section and create a knot, leaving the bare ends of the wire exposed.

7. Repeat with the other 3 pairs of strands.

8. Wire all 4 pairs of strands together to make a tree with 8 branches.

9. Thread the unbeaded wires through the hole in the folded card and secure inside the fold with Sellotape.

10. Splay out the branches and write the person's name on the card.

MATERIALS:

SHEET OF WHITE CARD
SCISSORS
A SHARP INSTRUMENT – A BRADAWL IS IDEAL
ROLL OF FINE CRAFT WIRE
TINY GLASS BEADS (FROM THE CRAFT SECTIONS OF DEPARTMENT STORES)
SELLOTAPE
SILVER PEN

Ivy-covered menu holders

A simple but really eye-catching way of presenting the Christmas menu.

1. Cover your work surface with newspaper, then lay down the ivy leaves and spray with metallic paint – bronze looks especially effective. Leave to dry.

2. Attach the "metallic" leaves around the frame with Blu Tack; they look best when overlapped.

3. Write your Christmas menu on a slip of paper and put it into the frame.

MATERIALS:

LARGE SHEET OF NEWSPAPER
FRESH IVY LEAVES
SILVER, GOLD OR BRONZE SPRAY PAINT
SOME BLU TACK
A SMALL PICTURE FRAME – PREFERABLY WOOD OR METAL

Vegetable tree

I can't be the only one who feels she's seen enough ornamental topiary trees to last a lifetime! However, this variation on the theme is really quirky and very attractive as a table decoration. It's also a good project for children to try.

1. Fill the plant pot to three-quarters of its depth with the pieces of oasis.

2. Take the dried-out corncob and stick it in the pot, wedging it firmly into the oasis. Cover the top with gravel or moss to disguise the oasis.

3. Take the florist's ball, soaked in water, and stick it firmly on top of the corncob.

4. Cut some cauliflower and broccoli into florets.

5. Take some small tomatoes and radishes, along with the cauliflower and broccoli, and pierce each piece of vegetable with a toothpick to create a stem.

6. Stick the stems into the florist's ball, arranging the vegetables as you wish and making sure you cover the whole of the ball.

MATERIALS:

PLANT POT, APPROX 20 CM (8″) HIGH, PREFERABLY TERRACOTTA
BITS OF OLD OASIS
OLD CORN COB
GRAVEL OR MOSS
FLORIST'S OASIS BALL, ABSORBENT
CAULIFLOWER
BROCCOLI
CHERRY TOMATOES
RADISHES
COCKTAIL STICKS
FRESH BORAGE OR MINT LEAVES

7. Finish off by slipping leaves of borage or mint in between the vegetables – they will create a lovely aroma.

Frosted Fruit centrepiece

A wonderfully extravagant-looking table centrepiece which always draws gasps of admiration. It is easy to prepare and the colours of the ingredients can be varied to suit whatever colour scheme you are following.

1. Prepare the fruit first. Wash and dry it to ensure that the skin is clean. Brush the fruit with a couple of whisked egg whites. Sprinkle thoroughly with caster sugar and leave to dry. The secret of successful frosting is to make sure that the whole of the surface of the fruit is covered in egg white and sugar, so that the fruit is completely encrusted and doesn't go bad.

2. Sellotape together the 2 blocks of oasis. Using a craft knife, cut 3 holes the same diameter as the candles in the centre of the smaller cake board.

3. Sandwich the oasis between the cake boards using oasis adhesive or a glue gun. Leave to dry. Through the holes, scoop the oasis to make holes big enough to accept the candles. Secure the candles by pushing them into the oasis.

4. Go right round the oasis inserting the dried flowers and berries.

5. Finish by piling the frosted fruit and candied peel on to the cake board. If the fruit is frosted properly the arrangement should last for up to a week.

MATERIALS:

VARIETY OF FRUIT, INCLUDING APPLES, ORANGES, LEMONS, GRAPES AND PLUMS
2 LIGHTLY WHISKED EGG WHITES
CASTER SUGAR
2 SQUARE CAKE BOARDS, ONE 25 CM (10") AND ONE 27 CM (11") ACROSS
2 RECTANGULAR BLOCKS OF FLORIST'S OASIS
SELLOTAPE
OASIS ADHESIVE (FROM A FLORIST) OR A GLUE GUN
CRAFT KNIFE
3 CREAM-COLOURED CHURCH CANDLES, APPROX 22 CM (9") HIGH
SELECTION OF PASTEL-COLOURED DRIED FLOWERS AND BERRIES
CANDIED PEEL (OPTIONAL)

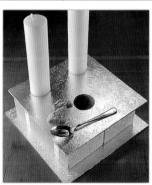

Sugar cube castle

Quite simply, this is one of my favourite ideas of all time. Building with sugar cubes is easy and non-toxic, and the finished product is just stunning. A must for the children to try – it will keep them busy for hours.

1. Position the 5 empty toilet rolls on the cake board, one in each of the 4 corners and the fifth right in the centre, equidistant from the other 4. These are the supports for the towers.

2. Pour the royal icing into a piping bag with a very small nozzle and start to build a wall of sugar cubes around each toilet roll, using the icing as mortar. The walls will be stronger if you imitate the positioning of bricks in real walls. Start with the tower in the middle and then work on the 4 on the outside.

3. When the walls reach the height of the toilet rolls, remove the rolls gently (leave in position if they resist) and continue to build the towers to your desired height. Leave to set.

4. In the same way, build sugar cube walls "cemented" with royal icing to link the towers together. Leave a gap at the front approximately 10 x 10 cm (4 x 4") for the drawbridge.

5. Turn the ice cream cones upside down and stick to the tops of the towers with royal icing. These are your turrets. Pour the glacé icing over them to resemble snow and then sprinkle with silver dust. Leave to set.

6. Build an arch over the opening at the front of the castle using a strip of thick card slightly wider than the opening. Cement it in place with royal icing and then build one layer of sugar cubes over the top to create the arch effect.

> **MATERIALS:**
>
> SILVER CAKE BOARD 37 CM SQUARE (15" x 15")
> 8 x 450 G (1 LB) BOXES COCKTAIL SUGAR CUBES
> 450 G (1 LB) ROYAL ICING
> 450 G (1 LB) GLACE ICING
> 2 PKTS EDIBLE SILVER CAKE DECORATING DUST
> 5 ICE CREAM CONES
> 1 WAFER FOR DRAWBRIDGE (AVAILABLE FROM DELICATESSENS)
> SILVER STRING
> 450 G (1 LB) ICING SUGAR
> 5 EMPTY TOILET ROLLS
> 200 G (8 OZ) GREEN ROYAL ICING (AVAILABLE IN TUBES READY-MADE FROM SUPERMARKETS)

7. Make the drawbridge by cutting a 10 x 10 cm (4 x 4") square out of the wafer. Use a cocktail stick to make a hole in 2 adjacent corners, thread a piece of silver string through each hole and knot so that it doesn't slip out. Next, cement the bottom of the wafer to the ground immediately underneath the arch, and then use the silver threads to lift the drawbridge and attach it to the tops of the walls above.

8. Use any remaining glacé icing to pour over the castle walls to create the effect of fallen snow.

9. Decorate the walls with spirals of green icing to resemble ivy.

10. Dust the whole castle with copious amounts of icing sugar.

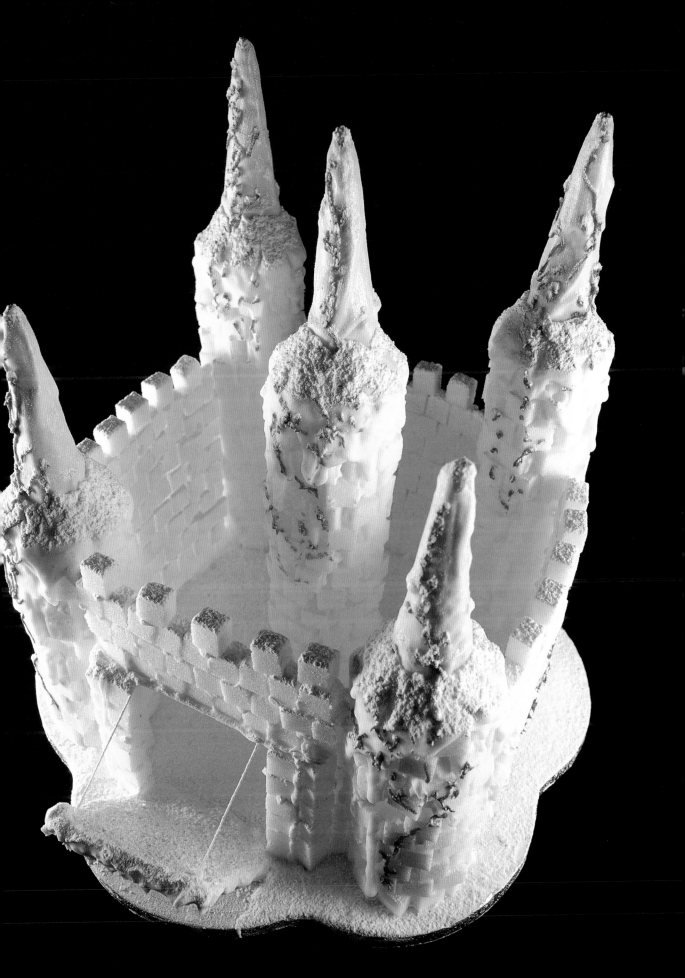

Byzantine tableware

Glass painting is easy to master and with a bit of imagination you can absolutely transform a plain dinner service at very little cost. Although the materials used are non-toxic, it is probably better not to decorate parts of the tableware that you wish to eat from. Always wash the decorated tableware by hand, not in a dishwasher.

MATERIALS:

ANY DINNER SERVICE – GLASS PLATES LOOK ESPECIALLY EFFECTIVE WHEN PAINTED

SELECTION OF MULTICOLOURED GLASS GEMSTONES (USE THE ONES SOLD IN DEPARTMENT STORES TO PUT AT THE BOTTOM OF GLASS VASES)

TWO-PART EPOXY GLUE (FROM ART SHOPS OR IRONMONGERS)

TUBE OF GLASS PAINT GOLD RELIEF LINER (FROM ART SHOPS)

SELECTION OF COLOURED GLASS PAINTS (FROM ART SHOPS)

BOTTLE OF CLEAR GLASS PAINT VARNISH

SELECTION OF FINE BRUSHES

1. Stick the glass gemstones on to the rim of the plates or the outside of the bowls using the epoxy glue. Leave to dry completely.

2. Use the gold relief liner to create patterns around the gemstones.

3. Next, use the liner to draw geometric shapes which you then fill in with coloured paints, creating a stained glass effect. Ensure there are no gaps in the relief liner, or the paint will seep through. Leave to dry thoroughly.

4. Coat the decorated area with clear glass paint varnish.

Initialled glasses

This idea takes seconds and adds instant glamour. Be careful not to apply the raw egg white too close to the rim of the glass, where people might swallow it.

1. Dip the paintbrush into the egg white, taking care not to put too much on the brush.

2. With the paintbrush, write the initial of the person concerned on the side of the glass.

3. Sprinkle caster sugar on the initial and gently shake off any excess, leaving the initial beautifully highlighted in white.

4. For a slightly different hue, put edible cake decorating powder in a colour of your choice into the sugar before sprinkling it on to the initial.

MATERIALS:

SET OF GLASSES
SET OF PLACE NAME CARDS
ONE EGG WHITE
SMALL PAINTBRUSH
BOWL OF CASTER SUGAR

5. The same principle can be applied to place name cards. Once again, be careful not to apply too much egg white, so that the card doesn't get soggy.

Candles and flowers

This is a great idea if you have to put together a table centrepiece very quickly, and it looks quite charming.

1. Soften the ends of the candles using a lighted match and secure them to the base of the glass bowl – you can use as many candles as you like, but I always think that one large one or three smaller ones looks best.

2. Half-fill the bowl with water, adding food colouring if you want to create tinted water.

3. Float the small candles on the water.

4. Sprinkle rose petals on the surface of the water.

5. Light the candles.

MATERIALS:

LARGE SHALLOW GLASS BOWL
TALL CANDLES
MATCHES
FOOD COLOURING
SMALL FLOATING CANDLES
ROSE PETALS

Recipes

Christmas is a time for being with other people, for sharing happy moments with family and friends. And good food is one of the very best ways to bring people together. A fine festive table is a guarantee of a happy Christmas.

Cakes, Sweets and Biscuits

This is probably my favourite part of Christmas cooking, because it's the perfect excuse to indulge my love of sweet things. Cakes, chocolates and biscuits are great "show off" items. Not only are they invariably easier to make than savoury dishes, but they have the visual "wow" factor and, lastly, there is almost always a willing audience to dispose of the proceeds!

Marbled fondant Christmas cake

Try this as an elegant alternative to the traditionally decorated Christmas cake. Marbled fondant is great fun to make, and the secret is to add only a little colour at a time, building up the marbling as you go along.

INGREDIENTS:
SHOP-BOUGHT FRUIT CAKE
SHOP-BOUGHT MARZIPAN
SHOP-BOUGHT READY-TO-ROLL SUGAR PASTE
SELECTION OF FOOD COLOURINGS (FROM SUPERMARKETS OR CAKE DECORATING SHOPS)
IRIDESCENT EDIBLE POWDERS (FROM SUPERMARKETS OR CAKE DECORATING SHOPS)
TOOTHPICKS

1. Cover the cake with a thin layer of marzipan as you would usually do before icing it.

2. For the marbling, mix tiny drops of food colouring dropped from the end of a cocktail stick into the sugar paste and knead until you achieve the desired marbled effect. Do not over-knead, as the colour should look streaky.

Good colour combinations are soft greens with silver dusting powder, gentle yellows with gold dusting powder and soft beiges with the merest hint of terracotta.

3. To ice the cake, roll out the sugar paste 7.5 cm (3") larger than the cake. Lay over a rolling pin and lift on to the cake. Use the palms of your hands dusted in cornflour to smooth the paste on to the cake.

4. Trim excess icing around the base of the cake.

5. Decorate with appropriate ribbons, e.g. light chiffon ribbon made into rosettes. Holly leaves can be cut from green net and outlined in coloured royal icing, or use any leftover sugar paste to make a few leaves, but don't overdecorate the cake.

Cardamon and soured cream fingers

Sophisticated Christmas biscuits for the real foodie. Makes 8 fingers.

1. Grease and line a 20 cm (8") square cake tin. Preheat oven to 180°C/ 350°F/ Gas Mark 4.

2. Open up the cardamon pods and extract the seeds. Grind them into a powder with a pestle and mortar.

3. Sieve the flour with the bicarbonate of soda and ground cardamon.

4. Cream butter and sugar until light and fluffy.

5. Gradually add the eggs one at a time, beating well after each addition.

6. Fold in the sieved flour and the soured cream.

INGREDIENTS:
250 G (9 OZ) SELF-RAISING FLOUR
½ TSP BICARBONATE OF SODA
24 GREEN CARDAMON PODS
175 G (6 OZ) BUTTER
250 G (9 OZ) CASTER SUGAR
3 EGGS (SIZE 3)
150 ML (¼ PT) SOURED CREAM

7. Spoon the mixture into the prepared tin. Bake until firm to the touch and golden in colour.

8. Turn out to cool. Cut into fingers when cold. Keep in an airtight container or freeze for up to 1 month.

Gilded ricotta tart *with winter fruit compote*

For some unknown reason, this tart always proves a hit with men! If you make your own sweet shortcrust pastry, you might like to add a little finely grated lemon zest to the mix. The following quantities make a 20–23 cm (8–9") tart.

1. Place the pistachio nuts on a shallow baking tray and roast in a preheated oven at 180°C/ 350°F/ Gas Mark 4 for 3–5 min, checking after 3 min (they go from brown to burnt in a matter of seconds). Set aside.

INGREDIENTS:
50 G (2 OZ) CHOPPED PISTACHIO NUTS
250 G (9 OZ) SHORTCRUST PASTRY
2 EGG WHITES, LIGHTLY BEATEN
350 G (12 OZ) RICOTTA CHEESE
3 EGG YOLKS
ZEST OF **½** LEMON, FINELY GRATED
ZEST OF **½** SMALL ORANGE, FINELY GRATED
110 G (4 OZ) CASTER SUGAR
3 TBSP DOUBLE CREAM
ICING SUGAR TO FINISH
EDIBLE GOLD LEAF (OPTIONAL)

2. Meanwhile, roll out the dough thinly and line a buttered 20–23 cm (8–9") loose-bottomed flan tin. Prick the base in several places with a fork and chill for 30 min.

3. Set the oven to 190°C/ 375°F/ Gas Mark 5. Bake the pastry case blind for 10 min – don't bother with paper and beans, simply check after 5 min and if any bubbles have appeared on the base, prick with a fork and press flat. Remove from the oven, brush inside with a little egg white and cook for 3 min more.

4. Reduce the oven to 170°C/ 325°F/ Gas Mark 3. Beat together the ricotta, egg yolks, lemon and orange zest and sugar until smooth. Stir in the cream and nuts. Pour into the pastry case. Bake in the centre of the oven for 45 min to 1 hour or until set and golden brown.

5. Decorate with gold leaf or dust with icing sugar.

Winter fruit compote
— to accompany the ricotta and pistachio tart

As a festive addition, what about this winter fruit compote? It is really warming and complements the tart perfectly.

1. Place all ingredients into a large heavy-based saucepan.

2. Bring slowly to the boil, stirring gently to dissolve sugar.

3. Turn down heat and simmer for 20–30 min.

4. Leave to cool down.

INGREDIENTS:
450 G (1 LB) ASSORTED DRIED FRUIT – THE PRE-SOAKED VARIETIES ARE BEST: TRY PEARS, APPLES, SLICED PRUNES, APRICOTS AND PEACHES
570 ML (1 PT) LIGHT RED WINE
110 G (4 OZ) CASTER SUGAR
3–4 CINNAMON STICKS
6–8 CLOVES
LARGE PIECES OF PEEL FROM **1** LEMON

Christmas nut Pavlova

Ever popular, this is a low-fat, nutty version of a Christmas favourite. It looks wonderful served on a large gold plate. Serves 6–8.

1. Preheat oven to 170°C/ 325°F/ Gas Mark 3.

2. Draw a circle 25 cm (10") in diameter on a sheet of silicone paper.

3. Whisk the egg whites in a large grease-free bowl until stiff but not dry.

4. Continue to whisk at full speed, adding the sugar at a slow trickle. When all the sugar has been added the mixture will be shiny and very stiff.

5. Mix the vinegar and cornflour to a smooth paste, then fold this mixture into the meringue. Gently fold in the flaked hazelnuts.

6. Spread the meringue on to the silicone paper circle, making sure that the edges are higher than the centre.

7. Transfer to the oven and immediately turn down the temperature to 150°C/ 300°F/ Gas Mark 2. Bake for 1 hour, then turn off the heat and leave the Pavlova for 2–3 hours to become cold, without opening the oven door.

8. Beat the cream until thick, add the crème fraîche and orange curd. Spoon or pipe the cream mixture on to the centre of the Pavlova and decorate with fruit of your choice.

9. Tips: the meringue base can be prepared ahead, wrapped carefully in foil and kept in an airtight container for up to 2 weeks. Alternatively, the finished Pavlova can be made up to 8 hours in advance. If you can't find flaked hazelnuts, slice whole hazelnuts on the fine-slicing disk of a food processor.

INGREDIENTS:

6 EGG WHITES

375 G (13 OZ) CASTER SUGAR

1 TSP WINE VINEGAR

1 TSP CORNFLOUR

175 G (6 OZ) FLAKED HAZELNUTS

175 ML (6 FL OZ) CRÈME FRAICHE

175 ML (6 FL OZ) WHIPPING CREAM

175 G (6 OZ) ORANGE CURD

225 G (8 OZ) FRUIT OF YOUR CHOICE E.G. PHYSALLIS, GREEN AND BLACK GRAPES, MANDARIN ORANGE SEGMENTS

Chocolate snowdrift cake

Dead easy to do, but looks very impressive – a snowdrift with a difference!

INGREDIENTS:
A CAKE OF YOUR CHOICE – A ROUND ONE ABOUT
20 CM (8") ACROSS LOOKS BEST
450 G (1 LB) BLOCK OF MARZIPAN
1 TBSP LIQUID GLUCOSE (FROM CHEMIST)
110 G (4 OZ) COCOA POWDER
LARGE SPATULA OR CAKE SERVER

1. Knead the glucose into the marzipan, add 75 g (3 oz) of the cocoa powder and mix until the chocolate colour is evenly distributed.

2. Roll out on a flat surface into a circle about 40 cm (16") across.

3. Mould the marzipan with your hands to create quite an exaggerated wavy effect.

4. Use the cake server to lift the marzipan on to the top of the cake and trim the edges, adjusting the "snowdrift" if necessary.

5. Dust with the remaining cocoa powder until all the marzipan is covered.

6. Display on a cake stand.

Illustrated opposite

Ten-minute truffles

A great gift idea – if they ever last long enough to be given away! Gift wrap in clear cellophane with an extravagant bow. Makes approximately 30.

1. Crumble the ginger cake in a food processor.

2. Add the remaining ingredients and fold to make a fairly soft mixture. If it becomes too soft to handle, chill until firm.

3. Shape into small balls.

4. Roll the balls in the coating while they are still tacky.

5. Place in petit fours cases or wrap in clear cellophane.

INGREDIENTS:
1 SHOP-BOUGHT 225 G (8 OZ) MOIST GINGER CAKE
110 G (4 OZ) DARK CHOCOLATE (MELTED)
75 G (3 OZ) DRIED CRANBERRIES, CHOPPED
1 TBSP CRANBERRY JUICE, RUM OR BRANDY

COATING:
2 TBSP SIFTED COCOA POWDER
2 TBSP SIFTED ICING SUGAR
1 TBSP GRATED DARK CHOCOLATE

Macaroon mountain

Children will absolutely love this fantasy cake and don't worry about the spun sugar – it isn't difficult to do.

1. Preheat oven to 160°C/ 325°F/ Gas Mark 3.

2. Line 3 or 4 baking sheets with non-stick baking parchment.

3. In a large bowl mix the ground almonds, flour, caster sugar, lemon zest and almond essence.

4. Slowly add enough egg white to make a soft but firm dough. Divide into pieces, rolling each piece into a rope as thick as a finger.

5. Cut the ropes into 12 graduated lengths. The first piece of "rope" should be about 10 cm (4") long. Fashion into a circle and place on a baking sheet. Make each consecutive piece of rope 2.5 cm (1") longer than the previous one, so that you create 12 graduated circles in total, the largest about 37 cm (15") in circumference.

6. Bake in batches for 20 min until pale in colour and firm to the touch. Cool on the sheet and then transfer to a wire rack.

7. For the icing, whisk the flower water and egg white. Gradually add the sifted icing sugar and beat well until soft peaks form.

8. Place the largest circle on a foil cake board and stick down with a little icing. Spread a little icing on the top of the circle and then top with the next largest circle. Continue until all the circles are on top of each other.

9. Use up the remaining icing by piping abstract stars on to parchment paper. Leave to set.

INGREDIENTS:
450 G (1 LB) GROUND ALMONDS
450 G (1 LB) CASTER SUGAR
25 G (1 OZ) FLOUR
1 TBSP LEMON ZEST, FINELY GRATED
1 TSP ALMOND ESSENCE
3 EGG WHITES, WHISKED
1 TSP ORANGE FLOWER WATER
1 EGG WHITE
200 G (8 OZ) SIFTED ICING SUGAR
50 G (2 OZ) CASTER SUGAR

10. For the spun sugar, put the caster sugar into a clean saucepan and heat gently until the sugar melts, then cook until you have a pale, light-textured caramel. Remove from the heat.

11. Using a metal spoon, lift a little of the caramel from the pan and dip the back of a fork into the caramel on the spoon, pulling the fork away quickly to form strands of caramel. Wrap these strands quickly around the tree. Keep on doing this until the tree is well coated. Press on the icing stars.

12. Serve within 1 hour of decorating. If you want to stand the tree for longer, omit the sugar spinning and decorate with icing sugar and a selection of frosted fruits, e.g. grapes, mandarins, cranberries and physalis.

13. If you find that the saucepan has set caramel stuck to it, do not try to scrape at it. Simply fill the pan with water, bring to the boil and the sugar will dissolve.

Christmas bombe

An adaptation of the classic Tuscan Zuccotto pudding, but I have given mine the Christmas feel by adding chestnut purée and chocolate stars. Serves 8–10.

1. Line a large mixing bowl with foil.

2. Melt the milk chocolate over a pan of hot water and allow to cool.

3. Mix the amaretto with the brandy and pour into a shallow dish.

4. Slice all the cake into strips, dip into the alcohol and then press them against the sides of the foil-lined bowl. Make sure no gaps are left, otherwise the filling will ooze out.

5. Whip the cream until stiff. Fold in the nuts, candied peel and sugar. Divide the cream in half.

6. Add the melted chocolate and chestnut purée to one half of the whipped cream.

7. Line the bottom and sides of the cake-lined bowl with the white cream, then use the chestnut chocolate cream to fill the hollow in the centre.

8. Level the top. Cover with foil.

9. Place the bowl in the freezer for 4–5 hours.

10. Melt the white chocolate in a bowl over hot water. Fill a paper piping bag with the melted chocolate and snip off the end of the bag. Pipe abstract stars on to non-stick parchment paper. Leave to set.

> **INGREDIENTS:**
> 50 G (2 OZ) BLANCHED ALMONDS, COARSELY CHOPPED
> 50 G (2 OZ) SHELLED HAZELNUTS, COARSELY CHOPPED
> 450 G (1 LB) MADEIRA OR SPONGE CAKE
> 6 TBSP AMARETTO LIQUEUR
> 4 TBSP BRANDY
> 1 LITRE (1¾ PTS) WHIPPING CREAM
> 150 G (5 OZ) SIFTED ICING SUGAR
> 50 G (2 OZ) MIXED CANDIED PEEL – FINELY CHOPPED
> 110 G (4 OZ) GOOD QUALITY MILK CHOCOLATE
> 110 G (4 OZ) CHESTNUT PUREE, SOFTENED
> 2 TBSP SIFTED COCOA POWDER
> 50 G (2 OZ) WHITE CHOCOLATE

11. To serve, remove from the freezer, unmould and gently remove the foil. Defrost for at least 4 hours.

12. Dust with sifted cocoa powder and decorate with chocolate stars. This dish looks particularly good presented on a very large white plate.

Party Food

Party food is fun food. It is an ideal chance to play with flavours, textures and shapes, the key being that the food should be both visually appealing and easy to eat. For parties, I also place quite a lot of emphasis upon vegetarian food, as I often feel that non-meat-eaters draw the short straw when faced with yet another plate of cocktail sausages and salmon quiche.

Ginger glazed ham with three pepper salsa

Party food can be very fussy and consequently unsatisfying. This, however, is a hearty dish that would satisfy any appetite. Serves 8–10.

1. Calculate the cooking time of the gammon according to instructions for boiling on the packaging.

2. Place the gammon in a large pot with the carrots, onions, celery and bouquet garni. Cover with water and bring to a simmer. Simmer for two-thirds of the calculated cooking time. Turn off the heat and leave in the cooking liquor until cool enough to handle.

3. Peel the skin of the gammon and transfer to a roasting tin. Preheat the oven to 190°C/ 375°F/ Gas Mark 5.

4. Mix together the sugar and root ginger. Score the fat on the gammon in a diamond pattern and press sugar firmly into the fat.

5. Spoon 150 ml (¼ pt) of the cooking liquid into the tin and bake the gammon for the remaining cooking time. Baste occasionally. Serve hot or cold.

INGREDIENTS:
4 KG (9 LB) GAMMON JOINT
2 CARROTS – CUT IN HALF
2 ONIONS – CUT IN QUARTERS
2 STICKS CELERY – CUT IN QUARTERS
BOUQUET GARNI
110 G (4 OZ) MUSCOVADO SUGAR
2 TBSP FRESHLY GRATED ROOT GINGER

Three pepper salsa

To be served with the ginger glazed ham.

1. Roast or grill the peppers until the skin is blackened. Put into a bowl and cover with cling film. Leave until cool.

2. Skin the peppers and chop finely.

3. Mix the peppers with the remaining ingredients. Leave in the refrigerator for at least 1 hour so that the flavours mingle.

INGREDIENTS:
1 RED PEPPER
1 YELLOW PEPPER
1 GREEN PEPPER
2 TBSP CORIANDER, CHOPPED
1 TBSP ROOT GINGER, GRATED
1 LARGE RED CHILLI PEPPER, DESEEDED AND FINELY CHOPPED
ZEST AND JUICE OF 1 LIME

Turkey and pumpkin raised pie

A real winter pie for hungry party people. Serves 8–10.

1. Grease a 23 x 5 cm (9" x 2") springform tin or a loose-bottomed cake tin. Preheat the oven to 200°C/ 400°F/ Gas Mark 6.

2. Mix the flour, herbs and seasoning to make the pastry. Melt the butter in a pan with the water and bring to the boil. Quickly stir in the flour, mixing to a soft dough. Cool slightly, turn out and knead briefly. Cover the pastry and leave to stand until cool enough to handle.

3. For the filling, mix all the ingredients together and season.

4. Roll out two-thirds of the pastry and line the tin.

5. Fill the pastry with the turkey mixture and press down firmly. Smooth the top.

6. Roll out the remaining pastry for the lid. Place the lid on top and pinch the edges together to form a seal. Make a decorative edge.

7. Make a slit in the centre of the lid to allow the steam to escape. Decorate with leftover pastry cut out into leaf shapes. Brush with beaten egg.

8. Bake for 1 hour, then very carefully loosen around the edges of the tin. Open the springform tin or carefully push the pie out of the loose-bottomed tin.

9. Place the pie on a baking sheet and brush the sides with the remaining beaten egg. Bake for further 30 min until well coloured, remove from oven and cool.

INGREDIENTS:
450 G (1 LB) PLAIN FLOUR
1 TBSP MIXED HERBS
SEASONING
150 G (5 OZ) BUTTER
250 ML (8 FL OZ) WATER

FILLING:
1 EGG, BEATEN, FOR GLAZING
600 G (1 LB 5 OZ) BONELESS, DICED TURKEY BREAST
450 G (16 OZ) MINCED BELLY PORK
275 G (10 OZ) DICED PUMPKIN FLESH
275 G (10 OZ) FRESH CRANBERRIES
2 CLOVES GARLIC, CRUSHED
4 SPRING ONIONS, CHOPPED
1 TSP CORIANDER POWDER
1 TSP GRATED NUTMEG
1 ORANGE, GRATED RIND AND JUICE
SEASONING

JELLY:
250 ML (8 FL OZ) BOILING WATER
1 TBSP SACHET OF GELATINE

---

10. For the jelly, stir the gelatine into hot water, dissolve completely, cool slightly and, using a jug or funnel, pour the jelly into the pie through the slit in the lid.

11. Cool before serving. Serve with cranberry relish or onion marmalade.

Illustrated opposite

Frozen fruit ring

A spectacular way to decorate a fruit punch.

MATERIALS:
METAL RING MOULD
CRUSHED ICE
SELECTION OF FRUITS SUCH AS GRAPES,
BLACKBERRIES, RASPBERRIES, ORANGE SLICES AND
KIWI FRUIT
2 GLASSES OF CRANBERRY JUICE

1. Line the base of the ring mould with a layer of crushed ice.

2. Place the fruits all around the mould on the crushed ice.

3. Pour the cranberry juice into the mould and place in the freezer for at least 8 hours or preferably overnight.

4. Take the iced fruit ring from the freezer and place it in a bowl of hot water for 15–20 seconds or until you see the edge of the ring beginning to melt.

5. Put a plate over the mould, turn it over and tap out the ring.

6. Gently place the iced ring in a large bowl of punch and watch it float.

Wild mushroom tart

Extremely tasty and a good party dish because it is so visual. Serves 4 or 8 if cut into party-size pieces.

1. Soak the dried mushrooms in boiling water for 20 min.

2. Mix together the butter, garlic and 2 tbsp parsley. Roll the butter into a sausage shape, wrap in foil and freeze or refrigerate.

3. Roll out the pastry on to a floured board to 25 cm (10") square. Place on a baking sheet. Brush the edges of the pastry with water. Turn over about 1 cm (½") of pastry all around the edge of the square, to create a small ridge. Prick the base and glaze with egg. Bake at 200°C/ 400°F/ Gas Mark 6 for 15–20 min until puffed up and golden.

4. Drain the dried mushrooms.

5. Melt half the garlic butter and sauté the dried and fresh mushrooms until cooked.

6. Place on the pastry case. Cut the remaining butter into discs and put it on top of the hot filling. Sprinkle with the remaining parsley.

INGREDIENTS:
10 G (½ OZ) DRIED PORCINI MUSHROOMS
110 G (4 OZ) BUTTER, SOFTENED
2 GARLIC CLOVES, CRUSHED
3 TBSP PARSLEY, CHOPPED
225 G (8 OZ) READY-MADE PUFF PASTRY
350 G (12 OZ) MIXED MUSHROOMS
1 EGG YOLK

Vegetable and sage fritters

Made with tempura batter, which is so light that you should hardly be able to see it.

1. Break up the broccoli and cauliflower into florets, blanch in boiling water for 2–3 min and refresh in ice cold water.

2. Deseed the tomatoes and cut into long strips. Pick the sage leaves.

3. Make the batter: break the egg into a bowl and whisk in the cold water. Add the flour, bicarbonate of soda and ginger, and beat very lightly for a few seconds (ignore any lumps).

4. Preheat the wok. Test whether the oil is hot enough by dropping in a cube of bread. If the oil is hot enough, the bread should brown in 30 seconds.

5. Dip the vegetables in the batter and fry until crisp, about 3–5 min. Dip the tomatoes in the batter and deep fry for 2–3 min. Dip the sage leaves in the batter and deep fry for 30 seconds.

6. Drain on some kitchen paper. Serve while still hot with a salsa, or flavour some shop-bought mayonnaise mixed with chopped coriander and lime juice.

INGREDIENTS:
450 G (1 LB) ASSORTED VEGETABLES – BROCCOLI, CAULIFLOWER AND PLUM TOMATOES
1 LARGE EGG
225 ML (8 FL OZ) ICE COLD WATER
110 G (4 OZ) PLAIN FLOUR
PINCH BICARBONATE SODA
1 TSP GROUND GINGER
ENOUGH VEGETABLE OIL TO HALF-FILL A WOK
BUNCH OF SAGE LEAVES
FLOUR FOR DUSTING

Spiced chickpea bites

Something a bit different from the traditional party snacks. Makes 20 small bites.

1. In a food processor grind the chickpeas with the onion, garlic and enough oil to help the blades work.

2. Add the spices and bread and blend until you achieve a firm consistency.

3. Using wet hands, form into small balls about the size of a walnut.

4. Deep fry in hot oil for 5 min until browned, or shallow fry for 4–5 min.

5. Serve with chutney and/or raita as a dip.

> **INGREDIENTS:**
> **400 G (14 OZ) CAN CHICKPEAS**
> **1 ONION**
> **4 TBSP OLIVE OIL**
> **1 CLOVE GARLIC**
> **1 TSP TURMERIC**
> **½ TSP CHILLI POWDER**
> **50 G (2 OZ) FRESH WHITE BREADCRUMBS**
> **OIL FOR FRYING**
> **MANGO CHUTNEY**
> **YOGHURT AND CUCUMBER RAITA**

Chestnut rolls

A brilliant alternative to the standard party sausage roll. These vegetarian rolls are absolutely irresistible, and they have the added advantage of freezing well. They always seem to be a particular hit with children. Makes about 30.

1. Mix together the chestnut purée, onion, garlic, lemon juice, soy sauce, breadcrumbs, chilli powder and pine nuts. Leave the mixture for a few minutes for the breadcrumbs to thicken, then add more if necessary to roll the mixture into small sausages.

2. Set the oven to 200°C/ 400°F/ Gas Mark 6.

3. Roll out the pastry on a lightly floured board to approx 30 x 30 cm (12 x 12") and, starting at the top, glaze a strip approx 7 cm (3") with a beaten egg.

4. Roll out one-sixth of the chestnut mix to a sausage shape and place in the middle of the 3-inch strip. Roll the pastry over the chestnut mixture and cut off the long sausage you have made with a sharp knife, pressing the edges firmly together. Cut into 2.5 cm (1") lengths, and place on a baking sheet. Cut slits in the top and glaze each roll. Repeat until all the pastry is used up.

5. Bake for 15–20 min or until the pastry is golden brown and crisp.

> **INGREDIENTS:**
> **2 x 350 G (2 x 12 OZ) PKTS FLAKY PASTRY**
> **435 G (16 OZ) CAN UNSWEETENED CHESTNUT PUREE**
> **1 ONION, GRATED**
> **1 GARLIC CLOVE, CRUSHED**
> **1 TBSP LEMON JUICE**
> **1 TBSP SOY SAUCE**
> **175 G (6 OZ) SOFT WHOLEWHEAT BREADCRUMBS**
> **½ TSP CHILLI POWDER**
> **75 G (3 OZ) PINE NUTS**
> **FLOUR FOR ROLLING**
> **1 EGG, SIZE 3, FOR EGGWASH**

Illustrated on page 83

Sesame nibbles

Just yummy! Makes about 40.

1. Preheat the oven to 200°C/ 400°F/ Gas Mark 6.

2. Brush one sheet of filo pastry with melted butter, keeping the rest of the filo pastry under a damp cloth to prevent drying out.

3. Sprinkle with 2–3 tbsp sesame seeds and 2 tbsp parmesan cheese.

4. Cut the pastry into 8 pieces and crunch each piece into a small ball, keeping the coated surface to the outside.

5. Place on a greased baking sheet.

6. Repeat as before and drizzle any remaining butter over the finished nibbles.

7. Bake for 10–12 min until crisp and golden in colour.

Illustrated opposite

INGREDIENTS:
5 SHEETS FILO PASTRY
75 G (3 OZ) MELTED BUTTER
15 TBSP SESAME SEEDS
12 TBSP GRATED PARMESAN CHEESE

Risotto balls

Filling and very "moreish". Everybody's favourite food bite sized! Makes about 25.

1. Heat the butter in a large, heavy-based pan, add the onion and fry until soft.

2. Add the risotto rice and coat with the butter.

3. Add the stock until all the liquid is absorbed and the rice becomes tender. This will take about 20 min. Season and leave to cool.

4. Put the breadcrumbs on a large plate.

5. Mix the egg, parmesan, paprika and parsley together thoroughly.

6. Roll the risotto mixture into small balls, dip into the beaten egg and then roll in the breadcrumbs. Chill.

7. Deep-fry the balls in preheated oil for about

3–4 min until golden brown and crisp. Drain and serve immediately.

Illustrated opposite

INGREDIENTS:
50 G (2 OZ) BUTTER
1 ONION, FINELY CHOPPED
250 G (9 OZ) RISOTTO RICE
900 ML (1½ PTS) HOT VEGETABLE STOCK
110 G (4 OZ) FRESHLY GRATED PARMESAN
GOOD PINCH PAPRIKA
2 TBSP PARSLEY, FRESHLY CHOPPED
SALT AND PEPPER
110 G (4 OZ) DRIED BREADCRUMBS
2 EGGS, BEATEN
SUNFLOWER OIL

Christmas Menus

Christmas meals and those who eat them tend to fall into two camps – the traditionalists and the modernists. It's either the full roast with trimmings or something completely alternative. I think it's very important to remember that Christmas means very different things to different people, and I always try to reflect this in the dishes I devise for the season. Above all else, there should be something for everyone, but not too much work for the cook!

Cinnamon duck with walnut and pomegranate rice

This is an excellent recipe. The pomegranate adds a really exotic twist, but if you don't like the sound of it, just make the cinnamon duck and serve with the vegetables of your choice (the red cabbage recipe goes beautifully). Equally, if you don't want to cook a whole bird, you can use just duck breasts, in which case simply cook them in the oven as normal and keep warm whilst you make the cinnamon sauce. Serves 4–6.

1. Roast the duck on a grid in a hot oven at 200°C/ 400°F/ Gas Mark 6, for approx 1½ hours or until cooked. Remove and break up into serving pieces.

2. Place the pieces of duck on a plate and keep warm.

3. Stir the pomegranate seeds and the chopped walnuts gently into the saffron rice. Keep warm.

4. Chop the onion and sauté in olive oil. Add the garlic and sauté until golden.

5. Add remaining ingredients and reduce until thickened. Season.

6. Place the rice on a warm serving dish.

7. Arrange the pieces of duck down the centre.

8. Pour the sauce over the duck and rice.

9. Garnish with pomegranate kernels and whole walnuts.

INGREDIENTS:
1 LARGE OVEN-READY DUCK
200 G (7 OZ) BASMATI RICE, COOKED WITH A PINCH OF SAFFRON
HALF A POMEGRANATE, SCOOPED OUT
25 G (1 OZ) CHOPPED WALNUTS
1 LARGE ONION, CHOPPED
1 GARLIC CLOVE, CRUSHED
150 ML (5 FL OZ) CHICKEN STOCK
150 ML (5 FL OZ) RED WINE
OLIVE OIL
1 TSP DRIED MARJORAM
1 TBSP DIJON MUSTARD
¼ TSP GROUND CINNAMON
2 TBSP REDCURRANT JELLY
SALT AND PEPPER
POMEGRANATE KERNELS AND WHOLE WALNUTS TO GARNISH

Vegetable terrine

A crunchy alternative for vegetarians – it also looks spectacular. Serves 6–8.

Health food shops and some supermarkets sell vegetarian alternatives to gelatin, such as Alginate and Caragreen.

1. Cook the pepper, courgettes, carrots and green beans in boiling, salted water for 3–5 min. It is important to drain the vegetables and pat them dry with paper towels.

2. Sauté the mushrooms in the butter until they are tender. Season and dry on paper towels.

3. Thoroughly butter a 2 lb loaf tin and layer the vegetables, sprinkling some of the cheese between each layer.

4. Mix together the cream, egg yolks, spices, salt and pepper.

5. Gently heat the gelatin or vegetarian alternative and stir into the cream mixture, then pour over the vegetables.

6. Cover the tin with foil and put it into a bain marie and then into a preheated oven at 170°C/ 325°F/ Gas Mark 3 for about 2 hours. It is ready when the sides are set, even if the centre is still soft.

7. Allow to cool. Refrigerate for several hours, then turn out and serve.

INGREDIENTS:
1 RED PEPPER, CORED AND CUT INTO STRIPS
110 G (4 OZ) COURGETTES, SLICED
225 G (8 OZ) CARROTS, SLICED THINLY LENGTHWISE
225 G (8 OZ) GREEN BEANS, TOPPED AND TAILED
225 G (8 OZ) BUTTON MUSHROOMS, SLICED
25 G (1 OZ) BUTTER
225 G (8 OZ) GRUYERE CHEESE, GRATED
425 ML (¾ PT) DOUBLE CREAM
5 SIZE 3 EGG YOLKS
½ TSP GRATED NUTMEG
½ TSP ALLSPICE
GOOD PINCH OF SALT AND PEPPER
11 G GELATIN (ONE SACHET) SOFTENED IN WATER

Vegetable jalousie

A wonderfully colourful vegetarian pie. Serves 4.

1. Heat the olive oil in a frying pan, add the carrots and cook gently, then slowly add each of the other vegetables and allow to sweat.

2. Add the garlic, coriander and seasoning.

3. Deglaze with the white wine and evaporate. Gently add the rest of the ingredients and allow the mixture to cool.

4. Roll out the pastry, fill it down the centre with vegetables, wrap over and cut slits on top.

5. Brush the pastry with olive oil. Bake at 200°C/ 400°F/ Gas Mark 6 for 25–30 min until well risen and golden in colour.

6. Serve hot with a fresh tomato coulis.

INGREDIENTS:
75 G (3 OZ) TINNED ARTICHOKE HEARTS
50 G (2 OZ) ONION, FINELY SLICED
1 CLOVE GARLIC, CHOPPED
50 G (2 OZ) CARROTS, THICKLY SLICED
175 G (6 OZ) AUBERGINE, LARGE DICED
175 G (6 OZ) COURGETTE, LARGE DICED
100 G (4 OZ) ROASTED RED PEPPER, PEELED
 AND DICED
1 TSP CORIANDER SEEDS, CRUSHED
3 TBSP OLIVE OIL
3 TBSP WHITE WINE
2 TBSP PARSLEY, CHOPPED
1 TBSP BASIL, CHOPPED
25 G (1 OZ) PITTED BLACK OLIVES
25 G (1 OZ) PARMESAN CHEESE, GRATED
450 G (1 LB) PUFF PASTRY
110 G (4 OZ) TOMATO COULIS

Scallops with minted pea puree

The wonderful colour of this dish makes it look particularly attractive – and the combination of flavours works well too. Serves 4.

1. Cut away the tough muscle at the sides of each scallop. Wash and dry the scallops well.

2. Toss the scallops in 1 tbsp olive oil and seasoning and set aside.

3. To make the pea purée, first blanch the peas and put to one side. Sweat the onions for 2 minutes, add the garlic and sweat for 1 more minute. Add the wine and reduce by half. Add the cream and reduce to coating consistency. Mix in the peas. Purée in a liquidiser. Keep warm.

4. Heat a ridged griddle pan until smoking, add the scallops and cook for 1 minute. Transfer to a plate and rest for 1 minute.

5. To make the dressing, mix the remaining oil, lemon juice and seasoning.

6. To serve, spoon some pea purée on to the centre of a plate, arrange the scallops on top, drizzle with dressing and garnish with mint.

7. The pea purée can be made in advance and can also be served with gammon.

INGREDIENTS:
12 LARGE SCALLOPS
3 TBSP EXTRA VIRGIN OLIVE OIL
1 TBSP LEMON JUICE
SEASONING
225 G (8 OZ) FROZEN PEAS
25 G (1 OZ) CHOPPED ONIONS
1 CLOVE GARLIC
150 ML (½ PT) DOUBLE CREAM
150 ML (½ PT) WHITE WINE
1 TBSP FRESH MINT LEAVES, CHOPPED

Cranberry-stuffed onions

A festive variation on the baked onion. Serves 6.

INGREDIENTS:
6 ONIONS
2 TBSP LEMON JUICE
4–6 TBSP VEGETABLE STOCK
25 G (1 OZ) BUTTER

FOR THE RELISH:
110 G (4 OZ) SUGAR
2 TBSP WATER
6 TBSP CIDER
GRATED RIND AND JUICE OF 1 ORANGE
350 G (12 OZ) CRANBERRIES, FRESH OR FROZEN

Illustrated on page 93, with Stilton Wreath

1. Parboil the onions in lemon juice and water (to just cover the onions).

2. Remove the central core using an apple corer. Place onions with stock and butter in an ovenproof dish, cover and bake for 25–30 min.

3. Dissolve the sugar in the cider, water and orange juice. Bring to the boil.

4. Add the orange rind and cranberries and simmer slowly until the cranberries are softened.

5. When the onions have cooled, drain and fill with the hot relish. Any leftover relish can be served separately in a warm dish.

Gilded goose

This method of "gilding" the goose dates from medieval times and gives the goose a gorgeous crispy golden coating. The same method can be applied to any bird.

1. Start to cook the bird as you normally would.

2. Gently cook the butter with the saffron until the butter turns bright yellow. Strain and remove the saffron strands.

3. Return to the pan and add the sugar and vinegar. Cook until syrupy.

4. Remove from the heat, stir a little of the mixture into the egg yolk, then pour all the egg yolk mixture back into the main pan (doing it this way prevents the egg from curdling). Continue cooking, without boiling, until thick.

INGREDIENTS:
1 CHRISTMAS BIRD
1 OZ (25 G) BUTTER
½ TSP SAFFRON
1 OZ (25 G) SUGAR
2 TBSP WHITE WINE SUGAR
1 EGG YOLK

5. Ten minutes before the bird is ready, remove it from the oven and paint with the gilding mixture. Return to the oven and continue cooking for 10 min.

Potato clouds

These will absolutely melt in your mouth – I first ate them in a hotel in France and practically begged the chef for the recipe. Makes approximately 30.

1. Preheat the deep-fat fryer to 180°C.

2. Bake the potatoes and when cooked, cut in half and scoop out the pulp, add 100 g (4 oz) of the butter and mash well. Season.

3. Boil the milk and add the remaining butter. Tip in the flour and beat vigorously. Remove from the heat.

4. Slowly beat in all the eggs so that the choux paste is of a dropping consistency.

5. Mix the potatoes into the choux paste.

6. Add the chopped herbs of your choice.

7. Deep fry tablespoon-sized lumps of the mixture in the hot fat. The potato clouds will rise to the top of the fat when they are ready – about 8 minutes per batch. They should be golden brown in colour, light and crisp on the outside with a fluffy centre.

INGREDIENTS:
6 LARGE BAKING POTATOES (CHOOSE A POWDERY VARIETY SUCH AS THE KING EDWARD)
200 ML (8 FL OZ) MILK
225 G (8 OZ) BUTTER
125 G (5 OZ) FLOUR
4 EGGS, BEATEN
SEASONING
2 TBSP FRESH HERBS, FINELY CHOPPED
VEGETABLE OIL FOR DEEP FRYING

Special red cabbage

One of my mother's recipes and a firm family favourite. It has a lovely sweet and sour taste. Serves 6.

1. Melt the lard and cook the onion.

2. Add the cabbage and sweat for a few minutes, stirring frequently.

3. Add the cloves, the bay leaf, 1½ tbsp wine vinegar and then slowly cook the cabbage over a low heat until it is cooked but still crisp, adding a little water to prevent drying out.

4. When done, sweeten with sugar and season to taste.

INGREDIENTS:
1 ONION, FINELY CHOPPED
1 COOKING APPLE, FINELY CHOPPED
MEDIUM SIZED RED CABBAGE, FINELY SHREDDED
6 CLOVES
BAY LEAF
RED WINE VINEGAR
SUGAR
SALT AND PEPPER
1 TBSP LARD

Stilton wreath with cranberry port sauce

An unusual vegetarian alternative to the Christmas bird. Serves 4–6.

1. Trim the leeks and remove any tough leaves. Slit the sides of the leeks and rinse them thoroughly under the tap, then cook the leeks in a large saucepan of boiling water for about 20 min, or until they are very tender.

2. Drain well – the water makes good stock for the sauce. Refresh the leeks under the cold tap and drain well again.

3. Trim any tough stems from the broccoli, then chop it into fairly small pieces (there should be 450 g (1 lb) after trimming.) Cook the broccoli for about 5 min in boiling water until tender, then drain.

4. Set the oven to 170°C/ 325°F/ Gas Mark 3. Grease a 1.5 litre (2½ pt) ring mould generously with butter. Lay single leaves of leek down the sides and base of the ring, going right round until it is all covered. Let the ends hang over the edge for the moment – don't cut them.

5. Chop the rest of the leeks finely and mix with the broccoli, stilton, cream, eggs, parsley, thyme, mustard and salt and pepper to taste. Pour the mixture into the mould – it won't quite fill it, but you need some space to allow the mixture to rise a little during cooking. Fold the overhanging leek leaves over the top.

6. Put the ring into a baking tin and pour boiling water around, to come halfway up the mould. Cover the foil and bake for 1 hour, or until the mould is set.

7. While the mould is cooking, wash the cranberries. Reserve some for decoration and put the remainder into a saucepan with the other ingredients. Cook gently for 5–10 min,

> **INGREDIENTS:**
> 700 G (1½ LB) LARGE LEEKS
> 700 G (1½ LB) BROCCOLI
> BUTTER FOR GREASING
> 250 G (9 OZ) STILTON CHEESE, GRATED
> 150 ML (½ PT) SINGLE CREAM
> 4 EGGS, BEATEN
> 1 HEAPED TSP ENGLISH MUSTARD
> 3 TBSP FRESH FLAT-LEAF PARSLEY, CHOPPED
> 6 TSP FRESH THYME, CHOPPED
> SALT AND FRESHLY GROUND BLACK PEPPER
> ROSEMARY SPRIGS (OPTIONAL)
>
> **CRANBERRY SAUCE:**
> 225 G (8 OZ) CRANBERRIES
> 2 PEARS, FINELY CHOPPED
> 4 TBSP WATER
> 110 G SUGAR
> 2 TSP PORT

or until the berries are soft but not mushy. Remove from the heat. Let the sauce cool and add the port.

8. When the mould is cooked, take it out of the oven and remove the foil. Loosen the edges of the mould, then turn it out on to a large round warm plate. If a small amount of liquid appears in the centre, blot it with kitchen paper.

9. Arrange the leaves of flat-leaf parsley and a few tiny sprigs of rosemary all around the top, to resemble a Christmas wreath, then arrange a few cranberries on top, at intervals, to resemble holly berries. Add a few cranberries and sprigs of rosemary around the plate (optional). Serve remaining cranberry sauce in a jug to accompany the wreath.

Minty pesto baked salmon in a crust

Traditional Christmas salmon with a difference. Serves 4.

1. Place 1 pastry sheet on a baking tray, lay the salmon on top and cut out a fish shape approx 2.5 cm (1") larger than the salmon.

2. To make the pesto, place the mint, pine nuts, garlic, olive oil, parmesan, lemon juice and seasoning in a food processor and blend. If it is too thick, add a little more oil.

3. Spread the pesto on top of the fish. Glaze the edges of the pastry with egg , cover with the remaining pastry and press down to resemble a fish. Make a scale pattern on the back of the fish by pressing the back of a teaspoon into the pastry. Glaze with egg and bake in a preheated oven at 180°C/ 350°F/ Gas Mark 4 for 30–35 min until golden.

INGREDIENTS:
800 G (1 LB 12 OZ) SKINNED WHOLE TAIL END OF SALMON
2 X 375 G PKTS READY-ROLLED PUFF PASTRY, THAWED IF FROZEN
1 EGG, BEATEN
25 G (1 OZ) FRESH MINT LEAVES
110 G (4 OZ) PINE NUTS
2 GARLIC CLOVES
125 ML (4 FL OZ) OLIVE OIL
50 G (2 OZ) FRESHLY GRATED PARMESAN CHEESE
1 TBSP LEMON JUICE

4. Serve warm or cold.

Golden couscous-stuffed turkey

Throw away the sage and onion and try this stuffing with a North African twist. The following quantities will stuff a 5–6.75 kg (11–15 lb) turkey.

INGREDIENTS:
150 G (5 OZ) COUSCOUS
50 G (2 OZ) BUTTER
1 RED ONION, CHOPPED
1 TSP CUMIN
1 TSP GROUND CORIANDER
1 TSP TURMERIC
150 G (5 OZ) CHOPPED ASSORTED NUTS
1 YELLOW PEPPER, FINELY CHOPPED
200 ML (8 FL OZ) VEGETABLE STOCK
1 EGG, BEATEN

1. Fry the onion in butter, add the spices and fry gently.

2. Add the rest of the ingredients and mix well. If the mixture is too dry, add a little extra stock. Allow to cool.

3. Use the mixture to stuff the turkey – if there are any leftovers, form into walnut-sized balls and bake separately until golden.

Red onion marmalade

Quite delicious – make a large quantity so you can give some away and keep some for yourself as a Christmas relish.

INGREDIENTS:
5 LARGE RED ONIONS
3 TBSP OLIVE OIL
GOOD PINCH SALT
GROUND BLACK PEPPER
3 TBSP DEMERARA SUGAR
4 TBSP RED WINE VINEGAR
350 ML (12 FL OZ) RED WINE

1. Peel and finely slice the onions, discarding the core.

2. Heat the oil in a wide-bottomed pan and cook the onions over a medium heat until soft, adding the salt as they cook.

3. Add the sugar and black pepper and cook until the onions become sticky.

4. Put the mixture into a smaller pan, add the wine vinegar and red wine, bring to the boil, reduce the heat and simmer until the mixture is viscous.

5. Allow to cool and store in a jar or in an airtight container in the fridge.

Index of projects and recipes